Also by Ilona Duncan

My Jewish Great Grandmother

At Home
On the Road

A Wayfaring Couple in North America

Ilona Duncan

At Home On the Road

ISBN - 978-0-578-60462-6

To Ian

Life has taught us that love does not consist in gazing at each other,
but looking together in the same direction.
Antoine de Saint'Exupery

Early one evening in 1997 Ian sat down in the family room of our Coral Gables home and said nonchalantly, "When I retire, we'll buy an RV."

I was peeling potatoes in the kitchen and heard words that didn't make sense. I looked up and saw my husband relaxing in his favorite leather chair, a can of soda in hand. From his grin I could tell he was watching for my reaction.

"What do you mean by RV?"

"A recreational vehicle to live in."

You must be kidding, I told him. But Ian wasn't joking. His idea was to spend two or three years exploring North America before shipping the vehicle to Copenhagen and traveling a year or two through Europe. I saw no point in discussing his silly fantasy and assumed that Ian was tired after his long flight from an overseas business trip. With his retirement a year away, I reasoned he would forget his outrageous plan.

Months went by without him mentioning it again. Then one Sunday morning, as we were having coffee and browsing the newspaper, he suddenly looked at me over the top of his reading glasses.

"What *do* you think of living in an RV?"

I put down the newspaper. "Seriously? You and I gypsies?"

"Why not?"

I wondered who had put the idea of an RV in his head. Probably one of his golf buddies. But Ian didn't relent. "Come on, Ilona. We'll visit places we've flown over for years." What places, I wanted to know. "The places we've seen from the air. Haven't you ever wondered what the country-side was like thirty-six thousand feet below?"

Before working as an executive for Airbus, the airplane manu-facturer, Ian had been a captain for Pan American World Airways. I'd been a stewardess from 1968 until we married and had children. Together we'd flown to every continent except Antarctica. I recalled how from the small window of an airplane I'd admired snow-capped mountains, islands surrounded by crystal-clear water, the South American rainforests, the African deserts and grasslands. Often, the enticing views made me crave to explore more. Still, I couldn't see us as nomads. As a child in Germany I'd seen small gypsy col-onies, called *Zigeuner*. These poor wanderers traveled in groups of two or three families on wooden wagons, which they parked on the outskirts of towns. I thought of my late mother and how shocked she would be. Her daughter on a *Zigeunerkarre*? I giggled at the thought.

"What's so funny?" Ian asked.

"I just pictured us touring the country in a roulotte." I'd chosen the French term for its sound, more befitting than its German coun-terpart.

"What's a *roulotte*?"

"French for a camper. Also a gypsy wagon with baskets and tin pots dangling from its sides."

Ian smiled. "I like that. *Roulotte*." As to the tin pots and baskets, he suggested I could learn weaving, satisfy my artistic nature, sell baskets on the road, and help with the cost of travel. I stared at him.

How did he come up with such silly notions? Yet Ian was ready to entice me. He described a roomy coach with a full kitchen and a large bathroom. I'd been in fancy boats with elaborate furnishings but never in a coach. I asked to show me such a vehicle. Ian vowed to take me shopping. Shopping? My husband did not like *shopping*. He must be serious, I thought.

Over the following months, we visited several dealerships and saw motorhomes of various types, designs, and sizes. The ones Ian liked were outfitted like luxurious yachts and bore no resemblance to a *roulotte*. Still, I had trepidations about selling our house and living permanently in such a vehicle. Could it turn into a terrible mistake? Would Ian really want to become a homeless wanderer after a long and successful career? People around the world thought highly of him. He was handsome at sixty-three. His dark brown eyes, charismatic smile, and gray boxed beard suggested a resemblance to Sean Connery. And would I, a well-educated woman who liked the arts and spoke several languages, embrace a nomadic life? In my younger years I'd been a model. I played piano and church organ. More recently I'd taught French, English, and German. I'd taken care of my appearance and was, at fifty-three, slim and attractive. What if I regretted the decision and ended up homeless? As I understood retirement, it meant to stop working and withdraw to a peaceful place. Ian disagreed. Retirement, he told me, meant the freedom to do what had been unfeasible while we worked. He wanted to travel, permanently.

I gave this thought, then suggested that we travel part-time and keep a small house. But where? Ian and I didn't favor Florida. We hadn't moved to Coral Gables by choice. Airbus, Ian's last employer, had relocated us there after a three-year assignment in France. I was definitely opposed to living in a golf community like some of our friends. Could it be that our journey would lead us to the perfect location where we would settle in old age? I recalled how much I'd enjoyed touring the United States with a friend by car in the summer of 1966. But I was young then, a free-spirited student who loved an unconventional way of life. Now, thirty-two years later, could I rekindle that abandonment and freedom? I rationalized that Ian and I always traveled well together. We'd been on outdoor adventures, floated down rivers in Idaho and Oregon, even camped in Alaska's wilderness. Still, an RV seemed an odd choice. I wondered if our youngest two children would feel abandoned without the place they called home. Ian didn't think so and said they would visit us and see different parts of the country.

Our twenty-year-old son, Alec, who studied at Embry-Riddle Aeronautical University in Daytona, thought we'd gone mad. Our daughter Natasha, the youngest and about to graduate from high school, considered the idea of an RV *cheesy*. Friends and business associates questioned our sanity. As I heard later, bets were placed on how long Ian and I could endure a restricted living space. But my loving, idealistic husband hoped that in retirement we could spend more time together and treasure the closeness that diminished during our hectic years of working. Was living in a bus a romantic notion? Could we make it work? Ian was confident we could. And eventually, so was I.

The hunt for our home on wheels became more serious. Ian scouted, tracked, and chased after the ultimate vehicle. In the past, when buying a house, I was the one who walked through a number of homes before narrowing the choices to four or five. Only then had Ian taken an interest. This time the roles were reversed. Ian spent hours with preliminary research. His vehicle had to be a sturdy coach with top of the line materials, good tires, a powerful generator, high capacity fuel and holding tanks. I didn't care about power and capacity. My prize winner would have a separate bedroom from the living area, large closets, and a big bathroom with a full-size shower. A new vehicle, the type Ian had in mind, cost over a million dollars, and was out of the question. Eventually, we chose a used converted bus. Love at first sight! Ian liked the strong, well-built chassis mounted on eight wheels, six in the rear, and two up front. I admired the interior lay-out, a mélange of extravagance and kitsch designed by the Marathon Coach factory in Oregon. Big closets, a spacious bathroom with walk-in shower, a side-aisle leading to the bedroom in back. The salesman suggested I sit in one of the cute round pink swivel chairs in the living area. I did, turned around, and said I was reminded of a ride at a fair. He took it as a compliment. I said in a convincing voice that I would prefer a couch instead. He seemed disappointed but quickly assured me that installing a second couch wouldn't pose a problem. Ian and I agreed that the vehicle fit all our needs. It was in perfect condition and had low mileage. The deal was done. We owned a bus.

In the spring of 1999, after many months on the market, our Coral Gables house was finally under contract. We had four weeks to downsize from a large four-bedroom residence to 350 square feet of living space on the bus. What to sell, what to keep, what to store? We debated, squabbled, and occasionally agreed on how to best dispose of furniture, china, holiday décor, books, tools, and accumulated knickknacks, some of sentimental value, some not. Ian, the frugal Scotsman, resented parting with his possessions, yet realized that the cost of storage would be higher than a particular item's actual value. My attitude was to rid ourselves of everything we hadn't used in recent years. Some pieces would furnish the Daytona townhouse we'd purchased for Alec's use. Others we shipped to Natasha's flat in New York City. Only furniture of value, artwork, china and silver would be kept in an air-conditioned storage facility. We were warned that beds, mattresses, and upholstered furniture would be unusable after years of storage. As to my piano, I searched for someone, hopefully a pianist, to house the 1917 *Gaveau* baby grand. My tuner had cautioned against long-term storage. Luckily, a friendly couple offered to take it if I paid for its upkeep.

A big concern was our five-year-old cat, Tanya, a beautiful, gentle Burmese. We'd watched her raise two sets of adorable kittens. Did she sense an upheaval? I thought of this whenever she looked at me with her big yellow eyes. Tanya loved the outdoors, climbing trees, lounging in flower beds. She would be miserable confined to a motorhome. We decided Tanya would be happier living with Alec in Daytona.

The closer we came to the moving date, the more the clean-out craze absorbed me. I sorted through our closets. Why had I kept fur coats? They served their purpose when we lived in Connecticut. Who would want them now in Miami? And what was I supposed to do with my sister-in-law's prom dresses with swinging skirts from the 1950s? A few years earlier, Natasha and her friends had amused themselves playing dress-up with lavish creations in bright pink satin, blue lace, and cream organza tulle. Then there were Ian's Air Force uniforms. Unless he lost thirty pounds, he would never fit into them again. Many items went to a consignment shop. With some regret I gave away shoes and handbags. More than ever before, I would be in Swedish clogs. Yet, I kept two pair of high heels, just in case, and a classy *Lancel* French handbag would become my day-to-day tote.

While I worked non-stop, Ian took time sorting through his things and told me not to act like a whirling dervish. He felt a nostalgic connection with documents from his Air Force career. Scanning through military orders from the 1950s, he relived episodes of his past. "Look at this," he would say and call me over. I told him he didn't need to authenticate his achievements, but might be interested in my latest find, a small leather crafted binder, the kind used to hold a notepad and pencil.

"What's in it?"

"Your love letters." I opened one, written on Pan American stationary, and began to read, *Dear Ilona, I've been drained of my energy thinking about you, missing you...*

Ian grimaced and asked to see the letter. "We need to burn them."

"No. What's wrong about a beautiful love story?" I decided to keep them, saying I might need to be reminded about that love at some future time. Now, twenty years later, I wonder if paper-written love letters are passé, outmoded by the use of electronic devices.

The day Ian saw me pulling folders and paraphernalia from a steamer trunk he got nervous. "Don't you dare throw away anything of mine."

"Of course not. Here you go." I placed cartons with binders in front of his chair. One by one, Ian picked through the contents.

"I can't believe we kept all this crap."

"I didn't. You did."

Out it went, into the garbage, together with his military orders, boxes of *Aviation Week* and decades of *National Geographic* magazines. But Ian insisted on storing his collection of golf logo balls, all eight hundred of them, and their wooden display cases, which decorated the walls in our laundry room. Today they hang in the garage.

We were both unwilling to part with books. Would I read again my collection of French and German literature? Would Ian ever look at the volumes on aviation? Still, books were old friends, which we hoped to revisit one day. We agreed to take a small assortment on the bus. But I did question holding on to several Pan American Operating Manuals and the fourteen volumes of the *Encyclopedia Bri-*

tannica. How could we have foreseen the Internet would make them obsolete in a short period of time?

We held an enormous garage sale and sold upholstered and leather chairs, a couch, tools, garden utensils, and holiday décor, which included the fake Christmas tree I'd reluctantly agreed to buy in Miami. Ian lamented the devalued prices of these items. The few belongings we decided to keep with us on the bus fit into a six by twelve foot trailer, which we towed behind our Jeep Grand Cherokee to the bank where our house closing took place.

Home is any four walls that enclose the right person.
Helen Rowland

We picked the bus up in Lakeland, Florida. The dealership had mounted a heavy plastic shield to protect the front of it and also added a towing apparatus. To familiarize himself with the vehicle, Ian went for a fifteen-minute drive with the sales representative. The advice he received was to make wide turns, watch both side mirrors, and check the back-up camera. Then on our own, we hooked the car to the tow bar, tested the electrical connection, and drove off.

A few minutes later, the bus was cruising along Interstate-4 with our Jeep Grand Cherokee in tow, altogether a sixty foot rig. Except for the customized large windows and a colorful painting of hot-air balloons on the rear, the forty-foot-long vehicle with stainless steel and blue trim could easily have been mistaken for a *Greyhound* coach. I'd settled in the passenger seat, a well-cushioned chair wide enough for two people. The manufacturer referred to it as a buddy seat that could swivel around and recline like a La-Z-Boy. I pushed a button to electrically elevate the footrest, put my feet on it, focused on the road ahead, and heard, "Comfortable, are you?"

"Very. Have you ever wondered about the origin of the term bus?"

"Not really."

"Comes from omnibus, in Latin, for all."

"I get it. Transport for many people."

"Not in our case. Should be the term *nobis*, for us."

"You call it what you want. Just don't tell anyone."

"Why not? Omnibus nobis. I like that. For all, for us."

"To me it's a bus," Ian said and suggested Latin be reserved for church.

"What's it like, driving this behemoth?"

"Nothing to it. Remember, I drove a Boeing 747." Yet Ian admitted his surprise that the bus handled so easily, even with our car in tow. "You should learn how to drive it."

"No. Never." I'd decided long ago that if Ian wanted to live on a bus, he would be my driver.

But he insisted. "I'll take you to a big parking lot and teach you."

"No. That's not going to happen. I'll be your navigator, tour guide, and homemaker." I'd already determined that the mechanical systems would be Ian's responsibility. The less I knew about the vehicle, the fewer arguments we would have.

"What would you do if we're somewhere in the boondocks and I have a heart attack?"

Why does he always have to imagine the worst scenario? A pilot, always a pilot with an alternative plan.

Finally I said, "If that happens, I'll figure something out," got up and sat on one of the couches in our new living room. Sliding my feet back and forth over the soft carpeting, I admired our new surroundings. The Wedgwood blue of the wall-to-wall carpet matched the blue leather on the driver's seat, dashboard, and seats in the dining booth. Heavy magenta silk curtains framed the windows, and double shades in pink could be set to semi-transparent privacy or to darkened interior. Mirrors adorned the ceiling and several crystal light fixtures provided full or indirect light. A television up front made me wonder if we needed the second one in the bedroom. Yet I knew this arrangement pleased Ian. Small glass enclosed wall cabinets would hold books. I'd opted to bring along the collected works of Goethe, twelve books bound in brown linen, a gift long ago from my mother. Maybe I would finally have the time to read them. I was pleased with the choice of our new home, without doubt the nicest of all the vehicles we'd seen. And it was custom-made, one of a kind.

Ian looked content in the driver's seat. Piloting the bus must be in his genes, I thought. He'd always liked commanding vehicles, be it boats, cars, or planes. Aviation had been his passion since the age of fifteen when he learned to fly at the Butler Graham airport in Pennsylvania where he grew up. He soloed at sixteen, was an instructor before becoming an Air Force Command Pilot, a Pan American Captain, and FAA designated Check-Airman. I trusted him. If he could navigate an airplane through bad weather and difficult traffic patterns, he certainly would be able to handle a bus. I, on the other hand, would have made a horrible pilot and panicked at the first sign of imminent danger. Creativity is my passion, I thought. I would decorate our new home, give it my personal flair, a bouquet of freshly picked flowers on the dining table, a potted plant on the counter in the galley or on the bar. But was there a way to keep the pot in place while we were moving? I would do some research. Maybe a few framed photos on the side table by the sofa?

The bus continued to move through traffic. Ian found a radio channel of country music. I got up from the couch, walked to the kitchen, opened a few cabinets, saw again the ample space for pots, pans, and dishes. I thought about the types of meals I would prepare on the Amana glass-top range. The microwave/convection oven was large enough to bake a cake, even roast a small turkey. And the garbage compactor would come in handy. Dishes would have to be washed by hand, an inconvenience despite the double sink. I pushed the faucet for instant boiling water. Why hadn't I brought teabags?

In the center of the kitchen was a twenty cubic foot two-door, side-by-side refrigerator/freezer and, suspended from the ceiling above the bar, a glass cabinet with crystal stemware. There was a trick to removing the glasses, as I later found out. This puzzle would serve as amusement for future visitors. Before walking to the rear of the bus, I asked Ian if he wanted anything to drink. My airline days came to mind. *Check with the cockpit every twenty minutes.* (That had been the rule at Pan American, particularly during long night flights to ensure pilots had not nodded off). I handed Ian the soda he'd requested. And he promised that we would never drive the bus at night. I believed him.

I walked the narrow corridor to the rear, passing the bathroom, its walls covered with mirrors. Gilded faucets decorated the sink and oversized shower. My daughter's term cheesy came to mind. Between the bath and bedroom was a closet to hang clothes, a rare feature in most RV's. In the bedroom, I lay down on the queen-sized bed and faced the mirror above. Could it get more kinky? I made the bed with the linens I'd brought along. It was going to be the first night in our new residence.

From now on home would be wherever our vehicle was parked. We weren't sure where the road would take us and where it would end. But we recognized our traveling would be less complicated: No more delays and check-in lines at airports, no more lost luggage, no search for hotels. I appreciated having my own bathroom at any time, and looked forward to freshly brewed coffee every morning before I got out of bed. Life looked good.

All you need is a plan, a roadmap, and the courage to press
on to your next destination.
Earl Nightingale

Our actual trip began July 2nd, 1999, when we left Daytona and drove north on Interstate 95.

"We're on our way, baby," Ian said, grinning like a young lad on his first adventure. He wore a gambler straw hat, tipping it occasionally to onlookers in passing cars.

"What's with the hat? You fancy yourself a film star?"

"No, but people think we are," he said, adding that he didn't want to disappoint them. Except for rock groups and film stars, few people drove a bus like ours. But I wasn't in the mood for joking that morning. Parting with Alec had seemed too final a good-bye, though we agreed to talk often by phone. When would I see him again? Ian noticed my sadness and asked what was the matter.

I tried to keep tears away and told him, "Nothing."

"Aw, come on."

"I hate saying good bye."

"You'll see Alec again."

I didn't ask when. Christmas? A birthday? The reality of being a permanent traveler had suddenly taken hold. Where would we be by the end of the year?

The final days had been hectic. With the bus parked in front of Alec's home, we'd loaded everything deemed essential: clothes for every occasion, dishes for six, pots and pans, silverware, games, cameras, a laptop, maps, food, my yoga mat, a case of biodegradable toilet paper, a product hard to find. A set of photo albums, souvenirs of our past, fit perfectly into a compartment under our bed. My selection of books and CD's were on board, so were Ian's golf clubs and fishing gear. The underbody storage areas were large enough to hold trunks with seasonal clothing, sporting equipment, a tent, an outdoor barbecue, and lawn chairs. And because we planned to live on the bus for many years, we carried filing boxes with financial records and other important documents. Paperless billing and electronic financial statements were not popular in 1999, although I was already paying our bills on-line, a novelty then. And regardless of our whereabouts, we still needed to file taxes. As to our mail, it went to Alec's address. Once a month he would forward it by overnight carrier.

"Put on some music," Ian said.

I selected a Mozart piano concerto. Uplifting yet pensive.

Ian had something else in mind. "I would rather listen to Willie."

I told him he could have Willie after Wolfgang Amadeus. The music brought solace, and I closed my eyes. In less than three hours Florida would be behind us. Would we ever return? How far would we be a month later? I knew how eager Ian was to hurry as far north as possible. A few short stays along the East Coast, visits with friends, then the rest of the summer in the Canadian provinces, to explore Newfoundland and Labrador. In 1999 the craze of owning recreational vehicles hadn't reached its peak of popularity, though they had existed in one form or another for over ninety years. We soon discovered that RV parks were seldom occupied and reservations could be made a day or two in advance. We also planned to stay in places not commonly visited. We'd seen big cities, stayed in luxury hotels, walked through the world's famous museums and cultural centers. Now we sought rough country, backwoods, and wildlife.

We'd been on the road a little over an hour, nearing Jacksonville, when Ian tried, unsuccessfully to call from our cellphone. His mood changed.

"The cell phone you chose is a piece of crap."

I played dumb. "It's not working?"

"No, it's not working," he said, sarcastically.

I knew he would blame me. I had chosen Omnipoint as our provider because it guaranteed coverage all over the USA, Canada, and Europe. But we soon discovered it was useless in most areas outside of big cities. Ian was convinced that any other phone company would have been more dependable. But would any have coverage in Labrador? The phone's unreliability would be a nuisance in months to come. Ian resented that people couldn't reach us. Wi-Fi and texting didn't exist. The only method to retrieve messages was to periodically call our cellphone number from a phone booth.

Though Ian was eager to reach Canada, he preferred not to drive more than four hours a day. Like a good pilot, he focused on getting the vehicle from point A to point B while checking on weather, traffic, and the instrument panel. He set a time for morning departure, calculated the mileage, the hours of travel, and planned for an on-time arrival. We didn't have a GPS, an IPhone, or some ingenious voice of navigation that called out the next intersection and turn-off. With the help of state maps and the AAA North American Road Atlas, I was the designated navigator who told Ian where to exit and turn. The second day on the road I asked him how he compared flying a plane to driving the bus. He said that flying was more relaxing. In an airplane, there was no need to look ahead several car lengths and worry about traffic flow. Air Traffic Control was in charge of that. Plus, he had the airline's mechanics and a hotline to flight operations available to help with maintenance and *en route* problems. In contrast, we were on our own, inexperienced greenhorns who couldn't anticipate the inevitable hurdles.

The first blunder occurred in Georgia at a gas station. After re-fueling, Ian realized our rig, all sixty feet of it, couldn't make the turn back to the road. Going in reverse was out of the question. He'd been warned never to attempt backing up with the car in tow. With a tone of urgency he told me to unhook the car.

"Hurry, people are behind us."

I'd already become a master at getting the car off the tow bar. Two minutes and it was free. In the meantime some impatient drivers, unable to reach the pumps, yelled and honked their horns. Ian slid open his window and yelled back. His words weren't pretty. I could tell he was becoming frenzied.

"Go and stop the oncoming road traffic."

I stepped out into the road, my hands held high, yelling for the drivers to stop, then signaled to Ian. Once he was on his way, I jumped into the car and followed. We stopped at the first opportunity to re-attach the car. Back in the bus, I noticed Ian's gambler hat on the floor. No doubt he'd thrown it. I could tell he was still fuming. The incident didn't fit with a pilot's sense of precision, and he blamed himself for the minor inconvenience he'd caused.

"Never again," he said. "Next time we'll go to a truck stop."

I didn't respond.

We spent the 4th of July weekend with friends at Hilton Head. Their home owner's association would not allow our parked bus near their house. We were directed to a designated area for motorhomes. It suited me fine, as we had the place to ourselves. While Ian played golf, I adjusted the shades to semi-transparency, stretched out on the bed with Goethe. Randomly I'd grabbed volume twelve of essays, maxims and reflections. While I leafed through the pages, a rose fell out, a flower I'd tried to preserve. Life had left it long ago, and the once bright red had faded. Still, even in this brittle state, the rose was beautiful. I read on the page. *Aus der Natur, nach welcher Seite hin man schaue, entspringt Unendliches* (From nature, whichever way one looks, leaps the eternal). How appropriate, I thought. Many times during our journey I would remember the saying. Could it be that I'd purposely placed the flower there? Nothing ever remains the same, yet everything is eternal. That night we watched fireworks: sudden bursts of sparkling colorful energy that momentarily lit the sky, then faded into nothingness.

The next day did not start well. The generator, our main power source, failed. A mechanic at a truck stop was unable to fix it. Rather than driving off, Ian pulled into a truck's parking space between two overnight haulers and called the factory. With a technician on the line, we stepped outside. While I held the phone, Ian lifted the door to the generator compartment, then tried for some thirty minutes to follow the technician's advice. The semi's rumbling engines alongside us drowned out the conversation. "Repeat, say again." I heard the words often. Scalding temperatures left clothing glued to our bodies, sweat was running down Ian's face. I alternated between wiping sweat from mine and holding my nostrils to avoid the smell of diesel. A few yards away a couple washed two dogs in a bucket. With envy I watched as the animals splashed in the cold water. Ian looked aggravated. I wondered if this house on wheels was not a big mistake.

The generator's problem wasn't diagnosed that day. But it worked intermittently, and we continued to James Island Park outside of Charleston, South Carolina. There, adjacent to a lake and amid trees and blooming shrubs, we let out the awnings, and set our outdoor table with a cloth and napkins. A ceramic container with flowers graced the kitchen counter. I'd discovered that modeling clay kept the pot in place even while the vehicle was moving. David and Edith, friends from Charleston, were coming for dinner. Ian grilled steaks, I made salad, baked potatoes. And, of course, there was wine and champagne to toast our new home. Our way of life enchanted Edith. She asked if there was a bed for her on the bus.

The day we left James Island, we opted to take route 17 North instead of the interstate. Traffic in Myrtle Beach was heavy. Two lanes of cars moved through town, drivers in a rush. I looked intently ahead to oncoming traffic lights. Stay green, green. At the speed we were moving, I fretted that our long and heavy rig would not stop in time should the traffic light change to red at the last moment. Ian did not share my concern. His jest motto was: We are bigger than the others, they'll stay out of our way.

In my seat, moving nervously from side to side, my feet against the dashboard, I readied to brace for a sudden stop. Yet the real reason for my concern was not a foreseeable accident. My home was in danger of being ruined. Ahead I saw the yellow light. Come on, slow down, Ian. It'll turn red any second. My thoughts didn't transfer. "Stop," I yelled loudly. Ian slammed on the brakes. With a jolt the bus stopped. Behind us, in the kitchen, the refrigerator doors opened. I heard jars and bottles crashing down.

"Why'd you yell? What's the matter with you?" Ian shouted.

I'd wanted to vindicate myself but broke out laughing, an involuntary reflex to lessen a bad situation. What could possibly be funny about the unsightly mess of broken eggs, spilled milk, open jars of pickles and garlic alongside streaks of Ketchup? Ian was not amused.

"Don't ever do that again. Leave the driving to me and shut up."

"Always my fault," I muttered, on all fours cleaning up. During our next stop we bought bungee cords to hold the doors of the freezer and fridge in place.

A day later, I enjoyed a bit of Schadenfreude. Back on the road after an overnight stay we heard loud pounding on the right side of the bus. Looking back, I saw the awning's arms banging against the windows. Other drivers had seen the canvas flapping and were honking their horns.

"Shit," Ian said and parked by the roadside.

I thought it was funny that he'd forgotten to secure the awning. Ian didn't laugh. Later that day we prepared a pre-departure checklist.

"I'm surprised you, the pilot, didn't think of this before," I teased.

Ian asked me to open the laptop and began to dictate.

Pre-departure Checklist
Disconnect all hoses and external connections
Make sure the portable water tank is full
Lock all latches on lower cargo compartments
Check tires for cuts and abrasions
Check engine compartment for leaks
Check that awnings are locked in place
Retract TV antenna (later became satellite antenna)
Secure doors of refrigerator
Store all loose items on counters, nightstands, sideboards
Review the routing of the day

At our next stop I printed the list and had it laminated. Ten days into our journey, we reverted to our professional duties of thirty years earlier. Ian, the pilot, referred to his laminated pre-departure checklist and, as he had in the past with airplanes, made his walk-around to check all outside hook-ups, tires, awning, and antennas. I, the stewardess, secured everything inside.

The time came to refuel again. With the last fiasco in mind, Ian pulled into a truck stop. After I'd given my credit card to the cashier, Ian started pumping diesel, set the handle to auto shut-off, and walked off to talk with a trucker. I stepped back inside the bus and closed the door. Filling the one hundred-and-fifty gallon tank took about twenty minutes. I'd lost track of time when the front door opened and I heard Ian yell, "Paper towels, quick."

A roll of paper towels in hand, I hurried to the door. Fumes of diesel crept into the bus. Ian was wading through it. How could one roll of paper towels help?

"What happened?"

"The automatic shut-off didn't work."

I urged Ian to throw out his shoes and socks, that he'd never remove the smell. He did so reluctantly. From then on, throughout our travels, we never refueled the bus without scouting out gas stations by car the day before.

The mechanical malfunctions continued. We were in Charlottesville, ready to depart one morning, when the engine refused to start. I had the foolish notion to ask Ian what could be wrong. He snapped, "Leave me alone."

I grabbed a book and walked away until I was out of ear reach, then sat down with my back resting against a tree trunk. I didn't see Ian walk over until I heard his angry voice. He was shaking the cell-phone at me.

"We're going to get another phone."

"Why?"

"I need to call the *Detroit Diesel* hot-line."

"What makes you think another phone works better?"

"Anything but this piece of shit."

Ian looked so angry that I feared he was going to smash the device. I suggested driving the car half a mile away to a hill where we had reception the day before. Reluctantly he agreed. And there, on a narrow country road beside a pasture, frozen in place to avoid losing the connection, Ian explained the situation to a technician. From what I overheard, there was an issue with the batteries and the starter. When the conversation was over, the only words out of my husband's mouth were, "Let's go."

Inside the car I asked, "What did he say?"

"You don't want to know."

I told Ian that I had a right to know what was wrong with our home.

"It has to be towed to an approved Detroit Diesel repair shop."

"Where would that be?"

"Harrisonburg."

I remained silent. There was nothing I could do about it. I didn't understand the mechanics of the bus, but felt we were jinxed. Only two weeks into our journey and we'd encountered one problem after another. Maybe our friends were right when they warned us about this adventure.

We waited all day for a tow truck. A little over an hour and five-hundred dollars later, our home was at the repair garage. We packed a small bag and moved into a motel. Two days later, the engine was running again, although the cause of the problem remained a mystery and would plague us in the future.

With some reluctance we continued our drive north. Yet Ian seemed optimistic. "We're learning. All part of the adventure."

"Not my kind of adventure," I mumbled. I'd been naïve to expect a trip without mechanical problems. The "learning" adventure continued on a highway in south New Jersey. Several cars passed us, drivers honking their horns. Ian ignored them. But the continuous honking made me nervous. "Something must be wrong," I said.

A car passed with a man's head out the passenger side window, his arms pointing to the back of the bus. Not the Jeep, I thought. Ian pulled over. We both got out, saw the shredded rear right tire, its rim exposed. The wheel must have hit the curb during a sharp turn in one of the small towns. We called AAA and waited. A state trooper, his lights flashing, stopped. Ian opened the front door and handed him his license and registration. The trooper asked Ian who he was driving for, and what he was doing in rural South New Jersey. Could he have a look inside the vehicle? I wondered if he was driven by curiosity or suspicion of drugs. Ian told the trooper we were a couple of retirees from Florida touring the country, showed him around, offered a soda, which he accepted with a smile. He took a seat in our living room. I served oatmeal cookies I'd baked the day before. Ian, delighted with an occasion to eat and make conversation, relished the company and cookies. By the time AAA arrived an hour later, the trouper knew the short version of Ian's life; that he'd grown up in Butler, Pennsylvania; that his parents were Scottish immigrants; that he learned to fly as a teenager, joined the Air Force, flew for the airlines, had five children, met me in Rome, and that now retired, we hoped to travel around North America in a bus. I still wonder if the trooper believed any of it.

A few days later on July 23rd we crossed the Verrazano Bridge on our way to Long Island for a weekend with friends. Natasha, who now lived in New York City, was going to join us. The heavy traffic that Friday afternoon didn't come as a surprise. We'd lived in New York and fought traffic before. In summer, thousands of New Yorkers head for beaches and their weekend homes. We knew that our tall vehicle would not clear the curved low bridges over the Southern State Parkway and opted for the Brooklyn-Queens Expressway. With its heavy truck traffic and vehicles as high as ours, Ian thought it was a safe alternative. Then a warning: All vehicles above 12 feet must take the next exit. Down the ramp we went into unknown territory, a seedy part of Brooklyn and heavy traffic. Ian wanted directions on how to get to the Long Island Expressway. Without a map of the city, I couldn't help. We were creeping forward, inch by inch. It took several light changes for the traffic to move through each intersection. Odd looking characters loitered near the curb. Ian feared that the Jeep wouldn't make it through Brooklyn. One of these strange fellows could unhook it in a minute. Nothing of the kind happened, and we found our way to the Belmont Lake State Park, a bucolic setting not far from our friends' home. There I could relax for a few days. Natasha joined us, eager to see our new living quarters. Our friends were disappointed that we wouldn't, as in the past, spend nights at their house. Despite all the problems we'd encountered by then, we preferred to be home.

For all evils there are two remedies...time and silence.
Alexandre Dumas

Ian and I had a penchant for time and silence. But for different reasons. When it came to the mechanics of the bus, he preferred to avoid any discussion that could influence his judgment. I thought a dialogue would facilitate a solution, even if I knew little about the mechanical systems. Four weeks into our travels, we were in Gloucester, Massachusetts, when the engine starter failed again. Ian brooded. I should have known better and ignored him, but asked if I could be of help. As before, he told me to leave him alone. I did, at the time. But recently, I asked Ian about the reason for his reluctance to discuss the mechanical failures the summer of 1999. He said my unsubstantiated opinion would have confused him and interfered with his way of thinking. And then he hadn't wanted to hear my complaint about another costly repair, when all he wanted was a well-maintained vehicle.

But that morning in Gloucester, after he noticed the damaged tire, Ian's taciturn behavior turned into crankiness. He paced around and scowled at me. I tried to make light of the situation, referred to his earlier comments about a learning adventure. He didn't want to hear it. I knew then to stay out of his way, took refuge in the bedroom, closed the curtains, grabbed a book, and propped myself up against the bed's headboard. Ever since my student days, I'd thought of bed as a sanctuary, a quiet place to read and study. And now years later, I relished the cozy bedroom in the bus. There I could ignore my husband's moods, the problems with engine starters, generators, and tires. Ian's demeanor didn't improve until the manufacturer, Prevost, sent a technician who, in Ian's words, had a brain. We had to wait for an overnight shipment of an equalizer for the main battery.

That evening after an early dinner Ian couldn't find anything suitable on television. The RV park didn't have cable hook-up. Only local channels were available. He sulked and threatened to have a satellite antenna mounted on the roof. He told me about our neighbor, the owner of a large Fleetwood RV, who had installed a special antenna at the cost of 7000 dollars so his children could watch television while the vehicle was moving. Sad, I thought, for the children to prefer daytime television and cartoons to the scenery outside. I told Ian I would never watch TV while he drove.

"Of course you won't," Ian said, "but I want to watch something besides local channels."

I wanted to say he was acting like a spoiled brat, but held my tongue. Ian's fetish for television wasn't new. In the past he'd turned it on the minute we entered a hotel room. Even in foreign countries he kept the sound on whether he understood the language or not. Palaver from television chat calmed him. I preferred the soothing effects of silence.

"Where will you get such an antenna?"

"At the Marathon factory in Oregon."

Oregon was a long way off. At the moment I needed a more peaceful place. The stress of the day was gnawing, so I went for a walk. A mile down the road I came to a cove, sat on a large boulder, admiring the scenery. The setting sun's rays colored homes across the inlet a golden hue and gave radiance to the drab reeds and grasses. Birds watching for prey settled on the brown banks. I welcomed the light breeze, enjoyed nature's stillness. I believe there is harmony in silence, that it balances inner chaos. Music depends on les silences, which the French call periods of rest in a score. Without them, a song would be continuous noise. I remained there, reflecting on the beauty of the moment until a noisy jet-skier dressed in a red shirt and blue pants appeared out of nowhere.

The following morning while waiting for the technician, I fetched my yoga mat from the storage compartment under the bed to do some stretches. By then, Ian should have gone outside to talk with a neighbor. But a light drizzle kept people inside their RVs. So he sat at the dinette table and studied a road atlas. I rolled out the mat a few feet from him. "Time for some yoga?" he asked. "Yes. You need to be quiet." Facing forward, I stood there, trying to rid my mind of all thoughts. Then I heard, "Ooooommmm," Ian's voice, a rich baritone, exaggerating the sound. I reminded him to keep comments to himself and started with a sun salutation. I stretched my arms upward, bent over, and lowered myself to the mat, slowly raising my upper body into the cobra pose. Although I couldn't see him, I sensed Ian's eyes on me. I should have known that it was only a matter of time before he would make a silly comment.

"Look at the cobra about to strike a mongoose."

"Shut up!" I bit my lip to refrain from giggling. "Isn't there anything you could be doing?"

"Don't worry about me. Continue."

"Can't you for once be quiet?" I stood up, took a deep breath before starting the routine over. I got as far as the downward dog position, pressed my shoulder blades together, my head almost touching the floor.

"Now we have a hunting dog after a rabbit in a hole."

That did it. I burst out laughing, lost my concentration, and curled up on the floor. Visibly amused over his remarks, Ian beamed.

Still trying to contain my laughter, I said, "What is it with you?" I'd always appreciated my husband's sense of humor but this was not the time for it. "Yoga isn't funny."

"Of course not. Oooooommmmm."

"The routines are hard enough."

"I can see that."

"Then look somewhere else."

I decided on a different pose, the bridge, and rolled over into a plank. Before getting back up I was again in downward dog.

"You should see yourself in the mirror on the ceiling. Butt up!"

"I told you not to look at me."

"I'm not. I'm looking at the ceiling."

"You're incorrigible. Go outside. Bother the neighbors!"

"I'd rather stay here and watch you."

"You won't anymore." I rolled up my mat. The bus, Ian's weird sense of humor, and yoga were incompatible. The next time I practiced yoga was at a studio.

Another cause for friction was Ian's concept of time. His brain was wired to a schedule. I should have known a pilot remains a pilot. In contrast, I hoped for spontaneity, to enjoy the moment. Ian, before going to bed, specified the time for departure the following morning. I considered his need for precision ridiculous. One evening, when he announced in his usual airline jargon, "Gear up at nine o'clock," I challenged him.

"Why precisely nine o'clock?"

"What's wrong with it?"

"I don't understand the rush." I wanted to remind him that we weren't working for the airlines any longer. Then a three-minute departure delay was a calamity. Yet that evening I decided to keep quiet since we were usually up by seven. The timer on our coffeemaker was set for 6:30 am. There would be no reason not to be ready by nine. Still, the rigid schedule annoyed me. Why can't he see it my way? We don't have to be anywhere.

Our routine each morning was to get up and have a glass of juice followed by coffee. I preferred to sip mine in bed and awaken slowly. Sometimes I wrote in my journal, other times I read a book. Ian preferred to sit at the dinette table and watch the news. After a quick shower I would tie my long hair in a ponytail, make the bed, wash the dishes, and place every loose item in its allocated place. (Dishes, pots, coffeemaker, toaster had to be latched in specially designed holders to prevent them from shifting while the bus moved.) Time permitting I would put on lipstick, mascara and eyeliner, although often I waited to do so until we were on the road. Ian, in the meantime, would have gone outside, lifted the door to a compartment near the rear of the bus, pulled the shiny chrome handles to flush the tanks, disconnected and stored the hoses. Lastly, we read the checklist out loud and were ready to go. As the bus rolled away, Ian looked at his watch and, depending on the time, announced *on-time departure* or the minutes we were ahead or behind schedule.

One morning a little past eight o'clock, I was still in bed when Ian came looking for me.

"Don't you think it's time you got up?"

His squinted eyes made me think he was either worried or testy. "I'll be up in a bit. Let me finish my coffee in peace."

"You can drink it on the road."

"No. I can't relax when you're driving."

"Next time get up earlier." His furrowed brow told me he was getting annoyed.

I didn't relent. "Why the rush? We don't have to be anywhere."

"I'm the driver, and I want to be on the road before everyone else."

I wanted to ask why the driver got to make all the decisions, but he'd left. I heard the door slam shut and stayed in bed a while longer. Would Ian ever be able to relax? Did he think time was running out? I thought about his initial proposal to travel two or three years in North America. And now he was fretting over minutes of delay. What if I hid watches and clocks? That morning Ian blamed me for leaving ten minutes behind schedule.

Far more stressful than an on-time departure was the arrival procedure. When it came to parking the bus at an RV park, Ian and I didn't speak the same language. Backing into a narrow spot was particularly tricky. Sometimes there was only a foot to spare on either side. Once, Ian hit a picnic table. Another time he narrowly missed a tree. This recurring crisis usually started after I'd unhooked the car at the entrance to an RV park, during which Ian went to register and pay. Then I followed the bus to our designated space and parked the car. Next I positioned myself behind the rear of the bus, ready to give directions. The longer the ordeal lasted, the more frustrated Ian got, and the more helpless I felt. I remember a narrow spot at an RV park in Maine. In back of the bus, I kept running from one side to the other.

With his head out the driver's window, Ian yelled, "You need to speak up and be where I can see you."

"I'm trying. But you don't hear me." I shouted the words over the loud clatter from the engine.

Ian yelled back. "Which way? Left? Right?"

"This way." I pointed my arm in one direction but the bus turned the wrong way. "Stop. The other way."

"What?"

"Wrong direction. Move forward."

"Jesus Christ, I'll look myself." Ian stormed out to assess the situation. At that point several owners of other campers had gathered, trying to get a close look at our vehicle. One of the men knew exactly what had to be done. More importantly, he and Ian spoke the same language. Glad not to be needed, I waited in the car until the bus was in place. Later I offered a solution.

"Why don't we buy a pair of long wands, the kind ramp agents use to park airplanes?"

Unamused, Ian asked why.

"Because that's what you've been accustomed to all your life. Maybe you'll be able to follow my directions."

Instead, walkie-talkies solved our problem.

Now almost twenty years later, I cannot fathom how an overnight delay or one minute past schedule were cause for hostility. The events seem silly and laughable now. And walkie-talkies to park a bus? Unimaginable by today's standards. Modern vehicles have automatic backup sensors with visual and aural alarms. And today Ian and I could have communicated by cellphones. Technology has changed so much. Yet I'm left with fond memories of that challenging time.

The four most beautiful words in our common language: I told you so.
Gore Vidal

It baffled me that a trash compactor could enthrall my bright, educated husband. The appliance, located halfway between kitchen and bathroom, had the appeal of an amusing toy. In passing, Ian frequently pushed the button that set the machine in motion. And with a devilish grin he looked at me while he listened to the crushing and banging sounds. Empty soda cans were his favorite. A single can made for instant entertainment. I usually shook my head at his infantile behavior and ignored him. But one evening after dinner when I was relaxing on the sofa, the machine just whined.

"What's going on?"

"I'm trying to get the compactor to work."

"What's wrong?"

"I can't open the damn thing." The whining started again.

"Stop playing with it."

Ian reset the circuit breaker. This didn't help. Now the trash compactor moaned. I got up and tried to pull the door open. It tilted two to three inches, which left a small gap at the top.

"I'm getting a flashlight," Ian said and went to the bedroom. He didn't return.

"Where are you?" I yelled. I'd taken a seat in the dinette.

"I can't find my flashlight."

"You have half a dozen of them. Look somewhere else." Ian kept flashlights in various compartments, including the cargo area. Not the petite kind that fit in a woman's purse. His flashlights were big and heavy with super-sized batteries. Ian reappeared empty-handed from the bedroom.

"Where did you hide it?"

"I don't touch your precious toys."

Ian found one by the driver's seat and said it wasn't the one he was looking for. He shone a light inside the compactor.

"Aha."

"What is it?"

"The ram's in the down position."

"What do you mean by ram? Can it be pulled up?"

"Forget it. You don't understand."

"No, I don't."

"See for yourself."

I knelt down in front of the compactor. Looking through the small gap, I saw a heavy screw about twelve inches long, wrapped in yellow plastic.

"A nice mess," I said. Part of the plastic garbage bag had wrapped itself around the power screw that pushes the metal ram up and down.

"Don't worry, I'll fix it."

"Your fault. You bought the wrong bags." I didn't need to explain what had happened. We'd run out of the manufacturer's recommended trash bags. But instead of waiting for a new shipment, Ian went to a local hardware store. The retailer didn't carry the correct size for our compactor, and Ian settled for a bigger size, a bright yellow heavy duty plastic bag.

I got up from the floor and wished Ian luck. But he couldn't slide his hand through the narrow opening.

"You try it. Your hands are smaller."

Again I knelt down, pulled on the door, and maneuvered my right hand through the gap. "I assume the circuit breaker is off."

"Yes. Can you pull on the plastic?"

"No, my fingers don't reach that far."

"Wait, I'll get needle nose pliers."

They didn't help. The plastic was so tightly wrapped around the screw that the pliers in my hand could not get a grip on the material. I suggested he get my tweezers from the bathroom. Then Ian stood next to me as I plucked strands of yellow plastic, one at a time, away from the screw. He asked. "Is it coming off?"

"Not as fast as you may think. You must have bought the toughest trash bags on the market."

Each small fragment of plastic took me several minutes. How many were there? Fifty? A hundred? I asked Ian to bring me a pillow so I would be more comfortable on the floor. The process might take hours. "Some mess you created, playing with your toy. You are going to pay big time."

Ian did not answer. With a hangdog expression he removed himself from the scene, sat on the couch, and watched TV. I tried to think of something malicious as repayment. An evening at the opera? Ian hated opera. Quid pro Quo. Or the symphony in Montreal or Quebec City? I took several deep breaths and continued pulling fragments of threads away from the screw.

"You have no idea how strong this stuff is."

"I'm sorry," Ian said, staring at the television.

"I told you not to buy the bags."

"Too late now."

An hour later I got off the floor to stretch, considered abandoning the task. Ian could take the appliance apart tomorrow. I pushed the thought away. He might create a bigger mess by dismantling the machine. Where would we find a repairman? At the next RV park? Back on the floor, I continued working, strange thoughts in my mind. Had someone told me twenty-five years ago, when I married, that I would end up living in a bus and pulling strands of yellow plastic from a trash compactor, I would have laughed. It was almost eleven o'clock when I heard, "How are you coming along?"

I told him not to talk. The later it got the more irritated I felt.

He asked, "Why don't you stop and finish tomorrow?"

"No." He was tired, ready to go to bed, but I knew he didn't want to leave me alone.

Four hours later, past midnight, the screw was finally free. I asked Ian to come over. As I opened the compactor, Ian said he owed me big time.

"You'll get the bill."

Thus ended Ian's infatuation with the trash compactor.

Today the event seems surreal. Could the trash compactor be a possible metaphor for marriage? Operated with diligence and handled with caution, not overloaded, not toyed with, it requires a strong bag to hold the trash, and periodically a new one. If overburdened, the mechanism may short out. Garbage compacted over time and not unloaded might burst. Has the ring of marriage, doesn't it?

Don't believe everything you see. Even salt looks like sugar.
Unknown

On Tuesday, the 10th of August, we opted to take scenic Highway 2 along a river in New Brunswick, Canada. Pristine countryside, beautiful farms, sweet white churches, few cars, and in the CD player Edvard Grieg's lyrical Morning.

"They say the world will end tomorrow," I said, referring to the total solar eclipse over southern England. I'd read crowds were gathering at Stonehenge, the visitors convinced something extraordinary would happen at eleven minutes past eleven o'clock the morning of August 11th.

"They will be disappointed. Nothing will happen. But you could have been put in jail last night," Ian said.

I tuned the music down and asked why.

"Remember the mace spray?"

I played dumb, knowing that I'd lied to the Custom's officer when we'd entered Canada late at night. She asked if we had any weapons and I'd answered with a firm NO. Flashlight in hand, she poked through closets and storage bins. Then she gave me a stern look and asked if I had any mace. I told her I didn't. Fortunately she failed to search the car where I'd hidden a can of this spray. Had she found the mace, I told Ian, I would have said it wasn't mine.

"Great, and put me in jail?"

"No one is going to jail," I said, wondering why Ian always imagined the worst scenario. Born self-righteous, everything black or white, right or wrong, no shade of gray with him. Was I wrong in bending facts once in a while? I turned the music back up and looked out over the countryside. Several minutes later, Ian asked what was planned for dinner. I hadn't given it a thought. And even if I had, I knew that Mr. Menu, as Ian was known within our family circle, would concoct his own culinary preference. He asked what was in the freezer. I wasn't sure but mentioned a few filets and some chicken breast.

"Chicken breast? How about chicken saltimbocca or cordon bleu?"

I noticed him grinning with delight but didn't favor his choices. "That means frying inside."

Ian must have detected reluctance in my voice. "What's wrong with that?"

"Stinks up the bus."

"That's why we have an exhaust fan."

I couldn't dispute his logic. The exhaust fan above the stove was powerful. Once, the fumes had reached a camper one hundred feet away. The owner had come over and asked Ian what was cooking. But that day on the road in New Brunswick I had a lighter meal in mind and suggested pasta.

"What type of pasta? Carbonara?"

I said I'll think about it. Just then we came upon a sizable produce stand by the roadside. For days I'd hoped for fresh greens and fruit. I asked Ian to stop and heard, "Hold on." In view of the short notice, not to hear Ian's usual protest surprised me. The tires skidded on the fine gravel of the parking area, dust flew, the bus stopped, I grabbed my purse, opened the door, and said, "Do you want to come along?"

"No. Buy whatever you want."

The market was under a big tent. Behind a check-out counter against a wall of gray canvas sat a middle-aged couple. The woman welcomed me. I was the only customer and took my time walking past counters laden with fresh produce. All appeared recently harvested. I didn't know where to begin. Looking over at the couple, I blurted, "Wow. This is heaven!"

The woman's smile seemed forced. *Did she wonder who I might be, getting off a fancy bus, calling her place heaven?* I walked back and forth, deciding what to buy, sensing her eyes following me.

"Would you like a bag?" the man asked and came forward. He wore a long-sleeve plaid shirt over jeans. A baseball cap shaded his face.

"Yes, please."

He handed me a large brown grocery bag. I placed salad greens, carrots, and spinach in it, then asked for a second bag. "It's been a while since I've seen garden-fresh produce like yours."

The woman, her folded arms on the checkout counter, could not withstand her curiosity any longer. "Where are you coming from?"

Would she believe me if I told the truth?

"Florida," I said and heard indistinct mumbling. My bags filled, I went to the cash register.

"How many in your vehicle?" the woman asked, adding up my bill.

"Just my husband and I." Did she wonder if we had a busload of people?

Pen in hand she looked up, visibly startled. "I hope you'll enjoy everything."

"Thanks. We will."

Back in the bus I placed the vegetables in the refrigerator.

"You think we have enough rabbit food for a while?" Ian asked.

"Maybe," I said, and added that some of it would make for a delicious pasta primavera.

"In a creamy sauce? With lots of parmesan?"

"Of course," I said, happy we agreed on the menu that day.

Years later, I don't recall the occasion, I mentioned the episode to friends. Someone said the couple at the produce stand reminded her of characters in a Hitchcock film. I disagreed. They were nice people, cautious maybe, yet curious. They wouldn't be the last. We didn't fit the usual RV crowd. Wherever we went, it felt as if people tried to categorize us. A couple alone in a fancy bus: no children, no dogs, no cats, a Florida license plate. Of course they wondered who we were. We sensed our actual story wasn't believable. Why not make something up? During one of our fuel stops, I noticed the inquisitive look of a female cashier. It couldn't have been my outfit. I was wearing my usual jeans and a short-sleeve shirt. I doubt she would have recognized the fancy French handbag over my shoulder or my Swedish clogs? I was about to walk out the door when she asked, "You're a musician, Miss?"

For a brief moment, the question took me aback. Then I turned around, smiled, and said, "Yes." Walking out I thought, not the kind you imagine.

Pop groups and rock bands toured the country in vehicles like ours. Did the woman think I was a rock star? Outside, I saw Ian gesticulating with a man while they walked around the bus. Another fan? I knew how much Ian enjoyed an audience. As if it were a sign of failure to remain quiet, he would talk and chat with anyone. I am the opposite. I seldom engage with strangers. This time was going to be different. Why not enliven the scene? The men must have heard my wooden clogs on the cement as I picked up my pace to the bus. I walked up to Ian, brushed strands of hair from my face, and said in a loud and firm voice, "I've told you many times NOT to engage in conversation with strangers."

Startled, the man stepped back. Ian remained calm and explained that the fellow was merely interested in the bus and hoped to take a peek inside.

"WHAT?" I turned to the stranger and told him that Ian was my driver and could not show the vehicle to anyone without my permission. Then I ordered Ian to hurry up.

"Yes Ma'am, right away." Ian bowed submissively, obviously understanding my ploy. He excused himself and told the man that he had to get back to *driving Miss Daisy*. From that moment on, as long as we were on the road, I'd be known as Miss Daisy.

What I don't understand is how women can pour hot wax on their bodies, let it
dry, then rip out every single hair by its root and still be scared of spiders.
                                                                    Jerry Seinfeld

On Friday, August 13th, Ian and I arrived in Antigonish, a small
Canadian university town in Nova Scotia, about one-hundred miles
northeast of Halifax. It had been six weeks since we'd left Florida,
and my hairy legs were in need of waxing. I could have started the
process of shaving, but using a razor had never appealed to me. At
the RV park, I searched the Yellow Pages for a beauty salon. The
Beauty Institute advertised facials and waxing, with same day appointments. I called the number. A female answered. I said I wanted
to make an appointment for waxing. She asked what I needed done.

"My legs."

"Can you be here at 6:30 tonight?"

Elated to have an appointment so quickly, I asked for the location.

"Inside the hospital, behind the chapel."

I'd already hung up when I thought about the odd whereabouts
and mentioned this to Ian. He said the location was strange, but perhaps the shop was affiliated with a health facility. He suggested we
take a drive after lunch and see if we could find it. An hour later, we
drove off in search of the hospital. On our way we passed St. Ninian's

Cathedral, an imposing Romanesque church dominating the center of Antigonish and overlooking the university campus. I pointed out the Gaelic inscription on the cathedral, Tigh Dhe (House of God) and reminded Ian that Gaelic used to be the language spoken in that part of Canada.

Ian was more interested in the name. "Who was St. Ninian?"

"One of your Scottish ancestors who attained sainthood," I said, teasing that this trait hadn't transferred to him. Ian asked how I could possibly think that.

A winding road up a small hill led to the hospital, a structure in red brick with several wings, a large parking lot in front of the main building.

"You think you will be able to find it this evening?" Ian asked.
I had no doubt that I could. But that evening, inside the hospital I was confused. The receptionist had left, the lobby empty, the lights turned off. Where is everyone? I returned to the parking lot and looked for another entry. All I saw was a sign to the Emergency entrance. Certainly not the place for a beauty salon. A young couple was about to get in a car.

"Excuse me, do you know where the entry to the *Beauty Institute* might be?"

"*Beauty Institute?*" The woman giggled and said she had no idea.

I walked back and stood by the door, contemplating what to do. Could I be at the wrong place? As I remembered the directions, I'd been told to drive to a hospital, enter the main door, and walk up the stairs behind the chapel. The chapel? There was no sign to the chapel. I looked at my watch. Six twenty-five. I worried about being late, went back inside, and decided to see where a dimly lit corridor would take me. A man appeared. A nurse?

"You seem lost," he said.

"Yes. I'm looking for the *Beauty Institute*."

"Are you sure it's here?"

"Yes, I've an appointment." I explained that I was a visitor in town and had been directed to come to the hospital. He didn't know about any Beauty Institute and suggested I go to the emergency room.

"Follow the hallway to the end. There will be an unlocked door, then turn left. Good luck."

I thanked him but felt ill at ease. Could the Beauty Institute be a hoax? At the emergency room, two nurses greeted me. One of them asked if she could be of help.

"I'm not sure."

"What's the problem?"

"I'm not sick. And it might sound strange. I'm looking for the Beauty Institute. I've an appointment for leg waxing."

One of the nurses looked puzzled. But the second said, "You want the morgue."

I'd been to many beauty salons around the world. But a morgue? "You must be kidding," I said.

"No, let me take you. It's above the chapel."

Once inside the chapel, she pointed to the far corner. "Go through that door and walk up the stairs."

I thanked her and hurried along, then remembered it was Friday the 13th. I entered the morgue and called, "Anyone here?" I had expected a dark room, not one brightly lit. Curtains for cubicle partitions were drawn back. A petite woman in her early twenties, not much older than Natasha, came forward and introduced herself as Anne.

"Am I in the right place for waxing?"

"This is it. Are you the woman who called this morning?"

I said I was and took a quick look around. A few stretchers but no sign of dead bodies. Anne asked me to follow her to a corner where I detected the sweet, resinous smell of heated wax.

"The wax is ready," she said putting on a white overall. Her dark hair was cut in short layers and framed a pleasing face with round cheeks and a tender smile.

"Sorry I'm late," I said, removing my jeans. "I had a hard time finding this place."

Anne asked me to lie on the gurney where she inspected my legs. "Lots of hair."

"That's why I'm here. But it's a strange place for a beauty salon."

"I'm the mortician and do this after hours" She smeared a big slab of warm wax on my right shin. I had the impression Anne thought the morgue was a natural location for this service. What type of body had lain earlier on the gurney, I wondered.

"Not too hot?" she asked, a reassuring tone in her voice.

"No, the wax is perfect." I closed my eyes, trying to unwind.

Within seconds she pulled away the slab of wax and with it masses of hair. Not a painful process. After years of waxing, it feels pleasant like a massage. Seeing no reaction on my part, she asked, "Are you all right?"

"Fine. Were you busy today?"

"Today was easy," she said, "only one body. On occasion I've had several customers."

"Dead customers?"

"Some dead, some alive."

I'd never thought about the work of a mortician and asked, "Do you wax the dead?"

She laughed. "No, but we use wax for cosmetic reshaping of the face." Smearing hot wax onto my other leg, she told me in repairing a body, she needed glue, wire, needle, thread, and lots of makeup. The process could take several hours.

I was curious why she had chosen this career. Before I could pose the question, she asked, where I was from and what had brought me to town. I told her that my husband and I were living in a bus and exploring the Canadian Maritimes. She had never heard of anyone traveling as we were and wanted to know where we were going next.

"Newfoundland. Then Labrador."

She asked me to turn over on my stomach. Applying hot wax to the back of my legs she asked if I liked cheesecake.

"I do, very much." I wondered if she planned on serving cheese-cake in the morgue.

While she pulled away strips of wax from my calves and thighs, she told me she'd baked a cheesecake that morning and was going to pick blueberries to make a topping. "You can come along. We'll enjoy it together."

I wondered if she felt sorry for me being homeless, or if she was just friendly and wanted company.

"Am I your last customer?"

"Yes," she said, rubbing oil over the smooth surface of my legs. "Would you like to join me picking blueberries?"

I said that I appreciated the invitation, loved blueberries, but it was getting late and my husband would worry. I didn't say I could not wait to tell Ian about my experience.

Given the same experience today, I might have accepted Anne's invitation to pick blueberries and eat cheesecake. Improved cell-phone coverage would have permitted a call or text to Ian, to let him know my whereabouts and well-being. I'd taken a liking to Anne. We could have shared stories and gotten to know each other. I would have been curious to hear how many women used Anne's services at the morgue. Like a dream, the event still seems surreal. If it weren't for my diary entries I might not trust my memory. A recent search on the Internet showed several Antigonish beauty salons advertising various services that include waxing. None are at the hospital. I wonder when the *Beauty Institute* ceased to exist.

The happiest man is he who learns from nature the lesson of worship.
Ralph Waldo Emerson

One day I said to Ian, "It is really so simple, to find the peace we crave nature."

These words weren't a new revelation, only a reminder of what we'd known all along. Ian and I shared a love for nature's fauna and flora. That first summer on the road, our happiest moments were away from cosmopolitan areas, the hustle of traffic and shopping malls.

On August 2nd, precisely one month after our departure from Florida, we drove by car to Wingaersheek Beach near Cape Ann, Massachusetts. We'd expected big crowds that morning; yet only a handful of people were gathered when we arrived. The receding tide exposed sandbars, the crystal clear sea beckoned us to wade in. I removed my sandals and urged Ian to follow me out. Ripples of water splashed my calves, and the soft sands undulated under my feet. Tiny shrimp were swimming by. Here and there a crab appeared in narrow grooves. Seagulls followed a few fishing boats that traversed a narrow channel and passed a lighthouse. I estimated that we could reach it in an hour if we walked past the dunes and rocks. Instead, we returned to the beach, placed towels on the sand next to a large boulder, and rested. With my eyes closed, I thought about the many beaches Ian and I had visited. How many years had it been? Twenty, or more? I recalled the times we played backgammon day after day on Bondi beach in Sydney, Australia. Ian had accused me of palming the dice. And I remembered fearless parasailing off the beach in Puerto Vallarta, or diving into the high surf off the African west coast.

That morning on Wingaersheek Beach I wished we'd brought a picnic and could spend the day there. Ian agreed that next time we would pack a lunch. We didn't return. But later in Maine, on a cloudy and cool morning, Ian didn't want to join me on Popham Beach. A drizzle began as I walked through the dunes past wild pink rosebushes and butterflies. Except for a few birds at water's edge, I was alone. Soon the rain increased, and I took shelter beneath a lifeguard post, sat down on the sand, and looked out at the gray, murky waters of the ocean. Two sailing vessels and a lobster boat disappeared from view. The rhythmic interval of waves coming ashore recalled a childhood vacation to the North Sea in Germany.

For a while I sat there, not wanting to leave, listening to the hurling wind and breaking surf. I recalled Cynthia, a slim and petite woman with shoulder-length blond hair. I'd met her on a pier near Gloucester, Massachusetts. We'd spoken only a short time, but I couldn't get her out of my mind. What is the force that allows strangers to suddenly connect? A gesture, a smile? That day in Gloucester I'd sat on wooden planks next to her and learned she came daily to the pier to meditate. Cynthia had lived in Gloucester since 1939. How lovely she must have been in her youth, I thought. She asked what had brought me to the area. I told her about our travels, our home on wheels, our children, Alec and Natasha. I confided how I missed them and how remorseful I felt for leaving them even though they were away in college at the time our adventure began. Cynthia told me her daughter had died of AIDS, and her husband, a fisherman, of a heroin overdose. He was not the only one. Lack of work frustrated fishermen in Gloucester. Drugs had made their way into bars. And she was recovering from a recent operation for stomach cancer. Yet Cynthia managed to smile. There was nothing dramatic about her, and she didn't appear to plead for sympathy as she told her story. Yet I detected melancholy in her eyes. Now, as I sat alone on Popham Beach, looking out over the ocean, I wondered how a person maintained such strength and courage.

It wasn't until Canada that Ian and I packed picnics and took day-trips away from our home. We watched the tidal bore at the mouth of the muddy Peditcodiac River in New Brunswick. On Cape George, Nova Scotia, under a cloudless sky, we ate at a picnic table behind the old lighthouse. Not another person there. I spotted trees full of red-cheeked apples down a ravine. Who had planted them? There wasn't a house nearby. Ian thought the climb up and down the ravine wasn't worth free apples. But I did and returned with a few. After lunch we hiked the short distance to the top of the cape. Eastern white pines, loaded with cones moved in the wind. The view over the water towards Cape Breton Island was spectacular.

"What a gorgeous day!"

"I ordered it just for you," Ian said.

I was happy to see him relaxed and enjoying the moment. Except for the breeze from the ocean, all was quiet, nature bestowing its peace. I don't know if I'd read it somewhere or made it up, that peace is to be in harmony with oneself, happiness to be in harmony with nature, and bliss to share both with another person. There standing on the high cliff looking out over the Gulf of St. Laurence, I felt that our adventure had created a deeper bond, reaffirmed the intimacy we once shared, and validated our belief in nature's sublime force.

I travel for travel's sake. The great affair is to move.
Robert Louis Stevenson

Our home remained in North Sydney, Nova Scotia, while we toured Newfoundland. Until then, I hadn't given thought to a vacation away from the bus, and it felt odd to pack a suitcase. As I saw it, our home was meant for travel, not to be locked up and left behind. But the cost of taking the bus on the ferryboat for a short twelve-day excursion was prohibitive, so we opted to take the car to Newfoundland and the islands of St. Pierre and Miquelon, the only remaining part of La Nouvelle France (the 17th century French North American colony), which France had retained to keep fishing rights near the Grand Banks.

On August 17th, we locked our home, left a key with the RV park's owner, and bade the bus farewell. The ferry left North Sydney mid-afternoon for a six-hour-trip to Port-aux-Basques.

Ian and I took a seat on the upper deck.

"Isn't our gypsy way of life wonderful?" I said, leaning my head against Ian's shoulder and relishing the sun. I'd expected rough seas, but the waters were calm. Only a few clouds dotted the far off horizon.

He placed his arm around me. "Couldn't be better. An everlasting holiday."

While we watched the coastline of Cape Breton Island disappear we reminisced about the past few days of touring Nova Scotia. Ian had been surprised the villages on the northern coastline of Cape Breton Island (Ile Royale in French) retained their French names. And, to show the loyalty to France, people had painted their houses in blue, white, and red, in honor of the French flag. We discussed the battles fought over the territory once known as French Acadia. I admitted how little I'd known about the plight of the Acadian people and their expulsion by the British, described in Longfellow's *Evangeline*. Ian talked about his Scottish forebears making the voyage in the late 1700s. Small ships like the 85-feet-long Hektor had carried nearly two hundred settlers on a crossing that took eleven weeks. Ian mentioned his great aunt who had come to Nova Scotia from Edinburgh in 1851 to be a schoolteacher but returned to Scotland after a year because she didn't like the Canadian winters.

"As if the winters in Scotland were much better," I said, "I think she missed her social life."

"I was told it was because of the Canadian winter."

"Come on, Ian, Edinburgh was a bustling city in the middle of the 19th century." I mentioned entertainment, family, friends. "What was there to do for a young woman in Nova Scotia in 1851?"

Ian shrugged his shoulders.

Cape Breton was fading to the west, its hilltops and coastline barely visible. I reminded Ian of our driving the Cabot Trail. Thick fog had concealed the road's elevation and vertical cliffs. But by mid-day the fog lifted, exposing small fishing villages along the rugged coast. "Remember Neil's Harbor?" I recalled our late lunch that day at a fishing shack by the water.

"Yes, good chowder, full of seafood."

"You would recall the menu," I said, "What struck me was the view." I'd compared it to an impressionistic painting: the ocean azure under a blue sky, the rocky shoreline golden in the afternoon sun.

But the thought of food awakened Ian's appetite. "Let's go inside and see what there is to eat here."

When we arrived in Port-aux-Basques, it was nighttime. I'd made a reservation at a motel advertised in the Newfoundland Tourist Guide. Yet the address didn't seem to exist. Except for the rare on-coming vehicle, we drove back and forth on the dark stretch of road, no-one to ask for directions, and our phone without signals. A faint-ly lit sign advertised a guesthouse. Could this be it? It was almost midnight. We entered a seedy bar. All over Ian's face was written, are you sure this is the place? A few scruffy-looking men, drinks in hand, looked us over. One of them showed us to a small sparsely furnished room with a bed, table, one chair, and two pegs on the wall for coats. It had the rustic touch I'd seen in Western movies. Ian didn't feel se-cure and lay awake most of the night. I slept in my clothes.

We left early the following morning. Unlike me, Ian had been to Newfoundland many times and wanted to revisit Ernest Harmon Air Force Base in Stephenville where he'd been based between 1958 and 1960 as part of an alert force to refuel Strategic Air Command jet bombers during the Cold War era. He'd been an Aircraft Commander on the Boeing KC-97 Stratotanker then.

That morning, while we walked past old hangars and housing, Ian told me how he'd spent two weeks every three months here, ready for an immediate launch. I asked about the flying conditions in winter.

"Horrific. Mountains of snow."

I tried to envision the behemoth of a tanker moving down the icy runway to the deep rumbling sound of its four propellers. "Did they have equipment to clean the runway?"

Ian said there'd been trucks to remove the snow, but the process could take several days. "Worst conditions I've ever flown in." Yet he seemed pleased that the buildings on base were well-maintained and housed a community college, that the airfield was still in use as a designated emergency landing site for the space shuttle.

My interest in Newfoundland dated back to landing in Gander while flying for Pan American. Strong headwinds on flights from Rome to New York occasionally required an unscheduled stop to take on extra fuel. I'd admired Newfoundland's unspoiled beauty then. Now, thirty years later, the countryside looked more dramatic than what I'd seen from the air. I discovered a geological wonderland with ancient rock formations, thick boreal forests, mountains, plateaus. There are no major roads through the center of Newfoundland. The Trans-Canada Highway makes a wide semi-circle from Port-aux-Basques to St. Johns.

On this leg of our adventure, we visited Gros Morne National Park and the Viking settlement of L'Anse aux Meadows in the northern region, explored the eastern shores, and stopped at Gander to visit the 1985 crash site of the Arrow Air DC-8 that killed all 256 soldiers on board. They'd returned from a peacekeeping mission in the Middle East. Ian had known the captain of that fatal flight, a furloughed Pan American pilot. The treeless slope where the plane burned was a sad reminder as was the Silent Witness Memorial, which shows a soldier standing on a rock and holding hands with a girl and a boy, each with an olive branch.

A week later, after arriving in St. Johns, Ian rethought our planned excursion to the French islands. "It's a full day's drive to Fortune. Then a boat ride."

I told him that I'd already made a reservation in a motel in Fortune and wasn't backing off.

"What do you think you'll find on the islands?" Ian asked.

"France." Since my student days in Paris I'd been enamored with the French way of life, their food and language. I'd thought of France as my adopted home and spoke French fluently, like a native.

Two days later, after an hour's boat ride, we reached St. Pierre, named after the patron saint of fishermen.

Once off the boat, through passport control, I felt I'd walked into *la Bretagne*. Peugeots and Renaults with French license plates lined the streets. French policiers whistled to get the traffic moving faster.

"How about a *café au lait?*"

"Yes, and a *pain au chocolat*," Ian said. We took a table outside a café and watched people.

A man in true French fashion walked by with baguettes tucked under his arm. And a *dame* dressed to be seen carried the typical French white pâtisserie box tied with a pink string. Only in France, I thought, and recalled how Ian and I had enjoyed living in Toulouse ten years earlier.

A local woman asked if she could join us at our table.

"Avec Plaisir." I asked her about the schools, retirement, and life in general on the islands. She told us how teachers, police, and government officials came on a two-year contract. Schoolchildren, after the age of fourteen, continued their education in Montpellier, a city in Southern France. She asked what had brought us to St Pierre. I explained that we were *des vagabonds, en movement permanent.*

She laughed, *"Comme les gitans."*

"Oui, gitans." Gypsies, I translated for Ian, and regrettably told

the woman we had to get going.

"*Bon voyage.*"

"*Au revoir.*"

A taxi took us out of town, past summer cottages and fields of horses, to the westernmost Cap de Brossard, a distance of little more than a mile. The driver said the town's people would move half a mile away for the summer. The new airport could accommodate an Air France Boeing 747 from Paris. The runway impressed Ian. I would have liked to stay longer, walk across the windswept rocky terrain, look out to sea. But the ferry wouldn't wait. Still I couldn't leave France without a stop at a *supermarché*. Ian and I walked back to the boat carrying bags of French paté, *foie gras*, soups, sauces, cornichons, mustard, jams, biscuits and French chocolat. A treasure trove, or as I would say in French, *un vrai trésor.*

The following morning we set out on the 600 mile drive back to Port-aux-Basques. We'd grown fond of Newfoundland and would have welcomed one more hike, to have cast more fishing lines, savored another piece of partridgeberry or bakeapple (cloudberry) pie. The countryside, wild and rugged, had satisfied our inherent longing for nature's beauty. And I would have liked to stay longer in St Pierre. Reunited with France on that windswept, forlorn island in the North Atlantic, I'd felt at home even if only for a few hours. Yet the bus was awaiting us, and new adventures beckoned.

Geography of Newfoundland and Labrador

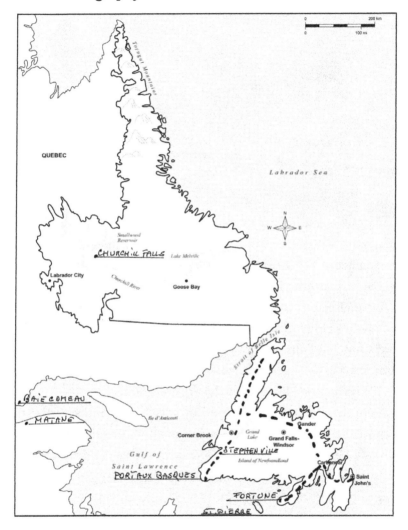

A nomad I will remain for life, in love with distant and uncharted places.
                                                          Isabelle Eberhardt

Ian was determined to travel to Goose Bay, Labrador. By car? Was there a road? I spread out a map on our dining table. A black, broken line, some seven hundred miles long, led from Baie-Comeau on the St. Laurence River north through Quebec, then west into Labrador, ending in Happy Valley-Goose Bay, the town's official name. Small dots along the way were Manic-Cinq, Gagnon, Labrador City and Churchill Falls. The road had to be the loneliest one in North America. I asked Ian who traveled up there.

"Who knows?" he laughed. "We're going to find out."

Ian's fascination with Goose Bay wasn't new. Years earlier, the airport there had served as a refueling stop for military and civil aircraft. On his way to Thule, Greenland, Ian landed Stratotankers at Goose Bay. And, because of weather, the occasional Pan American Clipper *en route* from San Francisco to London stopped there to take on extra fuel. Once I had been on the ground in Goose Bay when a snowstorm blanketed the Northeastern United States, closing several major airports. Yet neither Ian or I had seen more than the terminal building.

That day on the bus in August 1999, I closed the map and wondered if the long drive on a dirt road would be worth the trip. Earlier, in Newfoundland, I'd hoped to take a passenger ferry from St. Anthony to Goose Bay. But because the ferry served as a supply boat for villages accessible only by water, the voyage would have taken two weeks. Ian questioned me at the time and asked what I expected to see during the ferry ride besides seawater and native settlements. He envisioned a faster and more scenic trip by car. A new adventure, he called it. Despite our differences, we shared a love for distant and unchartered places. Ian was convinced that exploring was in his genes. Had he lived a few centuries earlier, he would have wanted to join a party of navigators. And I, given such an opportunity, might have studied the local languages and served as a translator.

In early September, we once again locked our home, and took a car ferry across the St. Laurence River from Matane to Baie-Comeau. We hoped to reach Labrador City before dark (370 miles) but that was quickly dashed. Thirty miles north of town, the paved road turned to gravel, which forced Ian to lower our speed to thirty miles per hour.

Narrow and uneven, the road curved along boreal forests, river-beds, and lakes. Often it made a steep ascent to a mountain peak before abruptly descending. Each time we approached the summit, I stretched as high as possible to see what lay ahead.

Ian laughed and said, "You act like a goose. The way you stretch out your neck."

I didn't like being called a goose and changed the subject. "Did you know Labrador was so mountainous?"

"Makes for a fun ride, no?"

I didn't miss Ian's facetious smile. Why did he take delight in my being a scaredy-cat? I wasn't always like this. In my youth I'd relished roller-coasters. And I hadn't been fearful when I rode the one at Tivoli Gardens, Copenhagen. I'd loved the Cyclone at Coney Island. I asked Ian if he remembered riding the roller-coaster in Munich at the Oktoberfest.

He chuckled. "We acted goofy then."

"We still do," I said, looking over a vast wilderness, untouched by man. "Only a goofball would be on this road."

The scenery didn't compare to anything we'd seen lately. Ten days earlier, along the Homestead Trail on Prince Edward Island, I'd watched a lively dance of white and yellow butterflies across a fresh-ly mowed field. Ian played golf that day, his only game that summer. I kidded him and asked if he'd bought a logo ball, showing Anne of Green Gables, to add to his collection. He hadn't. Sometime later, near the confluence of the Metis and St. Laurence Rivers, we visited the lovely *Jardins de Metis*, the 45-acre historic Reford estate with English-style gardens that the late Elsie Reford developed between 1920 and 1950. Roses were in bloom, their scent intoxicating and sweet, and I'd wished for a way to take the flagrance home. Our bus was at Annie's Place, a lovely campground in Metis-sur-Mer on the Gaspé Peninsula. I'd admired the quaint fishing villages nearby. The

day we went sightseeing, morning fog along the hilly coastline created a mysterious aura until the sun cleared away the mist and revealed small wooden houses by the seaside. Who lived there? Had
the residents traveled as we had? Been abroad? I recalled lunch at
a waterfront restaurant and a couple walking along the shore. Their
two young children skipped over the black rocks, followed by an orange cat with its tail in the air. The scene reminded me of a family
vacation at a beach resort in Nova Scotia. Alec and Natasha were
little then, seven and five. They'd splashed in the frigid waters during
our morning walks along the beach. Together we built sand castles,
then watched our creations disappear with the rising tide. Small
pleasures, happy memories. Ian put an end to my reverie. "What do
we have to eat? I could go for some of the tasty little shrimp we ate
yesterday in Matane."

"Fat chance," I said. "I would rather have *moules/frites* (mussels
and French fries) like we had in Mont Jolie the other day."
"I'll have that, too."

"You're such a gourmand." I opened the cooler, took out a sandwich, handed it to him. "This will have to do for now." I bit into an
apple.

The road continued up peaks and through valleys. Once or twice,
a cloud of dust from an oncoming truck blinded our view, forcing
Ian to stop. By two o'clock we reached the only gas station between
Baie-Comeau and Labrador City. Ian suggested I use the bathroom
but it didn't look inviting. I opted to wait until we reached Gagnon, a
dot sixty miles farther north on the map. Back on the road I watched
for wildlife, hoping to see a wolf or another wild creature. The animals didn't cooperate and, given the wide expanse of uninhabited
territory, I wasn't surprised. Ian was disappointed and said, "Will we
ever see something besides pine trees?"

Just then we met a sharp turn in the road and saw ahead a monstrous fortification that grew in size as we approached it. Ian stopped the car.

"Do you know what it is?"

"The guidebook says Manic-Cinq, the largest hydro-electric dam in the world."

The site seemed surreal, hidden away and surrounded by miles of forest. We stepped out and admired the imposing dam before Ian urged that we move on. By his calculations we were already behind schedule. Before long the lush-green landscape became a wide stretch of burnt territory. As far as we could see were blackened tree trunks. I asked Ian what he thought had caused the devastation.

"Lightning strike."

"Must have been some electrical storm to cause such a fire."

An hour later there was still no sign of civilization. "Shouldn't we be in Gagnon by now?" Ian asked.

"Yes. I really need a bathroom."

"What's wrong with the roadside?"

I said I'd wait. Just then the road changed from gravel to pavement with sidewalks.

"Looks like Gagnon is a ghost town," Ian said, pointing to foundations along both sides of the road where houses had stood. I didn't know we were driving on what had been Gagnon's main boulevard. Why were the houses destroyed? Whoever had torn down the town could have at least left a bathroom, I thought. Much later I researched Gagnon. It had been a large mining town with an airport, schools, churches, sidewalks, shops, and a hospital. After the mines became unprofitable, Gagnon was dismantled.

It was getting late in the day, the sun disappearing behind the horizon, painting the sky red. We'd been driving more than seven hours without seeing another car. Soon it would be dark. If the loose gravel damaged a tire, we would be stuck. By nine o'clock night surrounded us. With his hands on the steering wheel, Ian tried to follow a road that veered left to right, back and forth. "Hold on," Ian yelled as we bounced across an unexpected railroad track. The car's high beams hadn't shone far enough ahead to give fair warning

"Are you sure we're still on the road?" I wanted to know. We seemed to be on an undefined path of fine gravel with no shoulder. "I haven't seen an intersection."

"Not funny," I said.

We crossed another train track. Suddenly a faint glow brightened the terrain. Ian stopped the car.

"What's going on?"

"You want to see the Northern Lights?"

I'd been so focused on the road that I hadn't noticed them. We stepped out and admired bands of aqua blue and pale green flowing above. The Aurora Borealis wasn't new to us. We'd seen the spectacle before from airplane windows over the northern hemisphere. But that evening, on our way to Labrador, we had a private showing. I asked Ian if he'd ever thought how the northern tribes might have interpreted the colors. He hadn't. A year later in the Yukon, I learned the First Nation Peoples believed the flowing colors represented animals or deceased ancestors.

"Let's move on," Ian said, interrupting the magical moment.

The road seemed never-ending. We didn't understand why it meandered back and forth over railroad tracks. Then, lights in the distance.

"It must be Labrador City," I said.

Ian thought the lights weren't dispersed enough to form a town. He was right. Closer by, they revealed an enormous structure, several stories high.

"What in the world....?" Ian didn't finish his sentence. High-powered spotlights showed large vehicles in movement.

"Looks eerie," I said, "like a scene out of a James Bond movie."

"Strange stuff up here," Ian replied and kept driving. We learned later that the structure was a mine, which operated day and night. Shortly after eleven o'clock we knocked at the door of the bed &breakfast I'd booked in Labrador City. A cozy room was a welcome sight.

The following morning Ian was up early and went downstairs for breakfast. I wasn't hungry and had a cup of coffee in our room. On my nightstand was a brochure and map of the town. Was there anything particular to see? I scanned the booklet. Just then Ian came in and announced, beaming with excitement, that the owner of the B&B worked at the iron ore mine outside of town. "We'll be getting a private tour on our way back from Goose Bay."

"Wonderful," I said and began getting ready to leave. At one point I peeked out the window. On the street below, Ian was talking to a young man in black jeans and a dark windbreaker. I watched the man place his knapsack on the back seat. *It can't be. Ian is giving this fellow a ride. To where?* I grabbed my stuff, stormed downstairs, and waved Ian back inside. He followed me into the hallway and asked if there was a problem.

"Who is this person you were talking to?"

"A nice young man. He needs a ride to Goose Bay."

"You must be joking! We don't know him."

"Don't make a fuss," Ian said, explaining that the owner of the bed & breakfast had asked where we were going and wondered if we could take the young man along because he didn't have any money.

"Great. And you couldn't resist."

"What's the big deal? I agreed to take the guy to our next stop, Churchill Falls."

"What if he is some kind of weirdo?"

"Don't be so negative. It's only three hours to Churchill Falls."

That'll be a long three hours, I thought, and followed Ian back outside. The hitchhiker had already taken the backseat. Reluctantly, I sat in front of him. Ian introduced him as Mark Leland from the United States. I turned halfway around and gave this stranger a quick glance. He appeared to be in his mid-twenties, not much older than our twenty-two year old son, Alec.

There was an eerie silence in the car that morning, as we drove east of Labrador City. Even Ian, who is generally vocal, didn't say much. Imagining that our hitchhiker would dislike romantic Italian ballads, I put a disc of Andrea Bocelli in the CD player and stared out over the endless taiga, a term for the northern landscape, one I'd learned in a geography class. By the side of the road a beautiful wolf with a lush pelt and a long bushy tail broke the icy atmosphere. Ian stopped the car, but the wolf had places to be. It turned and dashed off.

Some sixty miles later, the driver of a broken-down eighteen wheeler waved us down. We all stepped out, Ian first, ready to be of help. "What's the problem?" he asked.

The driver said a rock had punctured the line to his airbrakes. Ian said he wasn't surprised, that the road was full of them. He offered the man a ride.

"I gotta stay with the truck," he replied.

"Why?" Ian asked.

"I'm carrying dangerous explosives."

Did I hear him right? Dangerous explosives? I quickly forgot my concern about the hitchhiker.

"What kind of explosives?" Ian wanted to know.

"Dynamite."

For the first time I looked straight at Mark, who reacted with a nervous twitch.

"Maybe we should get out of here," he said.

"Yes, hurry up Ian, let's go!"

But Ian, the Good Samaritan, asked if there was anything he could do. The trucker explained that his satellite phone couldn't get a signal at that location. He asked Ian to call his dispatcher from a phone booth in Churchill Falls and ask him to send a helicopter with parts.

"Sure can," Ian said, and took the toll-free phone number.

Back in the car, we speculated how long it would be before a helicopter delivered the part. Three hours? Four? Where would the part come from? Goose Bay? Ian wondered where the nearest phone booth might be.

By noon we reached the small settlement of Churchill Falls and drove around in search of the motel I'd seen advertised in the Labrador tourist guide. All we saw were shabby prefabricated houses. Not one resembled a motel. Ian suggested I inquire inside the community hall, an expansive building which, as I soon discovered, held under one roof the local Post Office, Town Hall, a school, library, a restaurant, and motel. Not the type of accommodation I'd expected. While I checked in, Ian located a phone booth and contacted the trucking company's dispatcher. Outside, Mark pitched a tent on the lawn. To get to our room, we crossed a communal area and bar, crowded with men. Their lustful looks made me feel uncomfortable. Didn't they have anything else to do but lounge around a bar and check out the only woman passing through? Later we heard they were striking laborers from the power station.

The community of Churchill Falls belongs to the hydro-electric power plant, and Ian hoped for a tour. But the strike cancelled that plan. Instead we asked for directions to the falls or what was left of them. Thirty years earlier, the course of the mighty Churchill River had been redirected to an underground power plant. We were told to look for a path by a narrow bridge a few miles outside of town. The site was not obvious. Several times we drove back and forth on the same stretch of road. Eventually, the driver of a road grader helped us find it.

"You're going out there alone?" The man's tone of voice suggested we were nuts.

"Is there a reason we shouldn't?" I asked.

The man shrugged his shoulders and slowly moved on, the grader's blades scraping over the gravel. We locked the car, and walked off into the woods. Soft yellow, lime green, and burnt orange moss covered the ground. I welcomed the familiar scent of spruces and pines, and marveled at the lack of insects. Fallen tree trunks and rivulets made the trail difficult to follow. We lost track of time. Suddenly Ian stopped. "Listen."

"What?"

"The roar. It's the falls."

We continued our hike in the direction of the noise. Along the way I picked a few blueberries. "Should we look out for bears?"

"You make enough noise to scare them away," Ian said.

We didn't need to have worried. Later that day we saw that bears had enough to eat at the local garbage dump.

As we passed through marshes, climbed over rocks, balanced on a log to cross a creek, Ian wondered why anyone would want to fight the crowds in Yellowstone when the best of nature was here. I said that few people were as crazy as we were, venturing out alone in the wilderness of Labrador in search of what used to be a waterfall. Yet, the sight was impressive: a chute of solid rock, two hundred feet wide, smoothed out after years of erosion. Anyone stepping out onto the polished surface would slide down a 1000 feet drop.

I shouted over the thundering roar of water below, "Can you imagine how magnificent this must have looked forty years ago?" For a while we stood there, in awe. I took a few photos. Ian said the site reminded him of Victoria Falls in Africa, one of nature's great wonders, and I agreed.

The following morning, as if preplanned, Mark stood at exactly the same spot by the road where we'd left him the day before. It had been raining all night. He looked cold and miserable.

"Hop in," Ian said.

I didn't protest. Mark looked relieved to be in a warm car. His presence didn't bother me anymore. Instead, I tried to figure out who this young man was. Of medium height and an athletic build, he wasn't unattractive. But with his dark, disheveled hair extending down his neck, he could have passed for a polite and well-spoken hippy. What could have prompted him to hitchhike in this remote territory? I had to ask. Between Churchill Falls and Goose Bay, Mark told us about his well-to-do family. We heard about parental disciplinary issues and how he'd flunked out of college. A psychologist had urged him to travel on his own with limited funds to areas where he could find peace within himself. Was any of it true? The road less traveled came to mind, a cliché for a pilgrimage of self-discovery.

That day, in early September, the temperature reached eighty-five degrees in Happy Valley, Goose Bay. People in bathing suits were eating ice-cream. Mark was vague about the length of his stay. We wished him luck. Ian and I visited the airport and military museum. The town didn't have much else to offer, so we decided to leave the following morning. Mark must have thought the same. We found him on the outskirts of town, hoping for a ride. He must have ESP, I thought. By then I wasn't sure if I should feel sorry or happy for Mark. Was he lonely? Hungry? I offered him one of our sandwiches. A mother's instinct. He gratefully accepted. My thoughts went to Alec. What if he were alone and hitchhiking penniless through Labrador? But I knew it wasn't my son's style. Natasha might be impulsive enough to do this. She had her father's sense of adventure and my spirit. I wondered if Mark's parents even knew where he was.

Back in Labrador City, Ian and I enjoyed our personal tour of the iron ore mine, which we were told was the largest in the world with one billion tons of iron mined. The giant trucks intrigued me. Next to them, our car resembled a matchbox toy that didn't reach half the height of their tires. I spent the remainder of the day at the library, reading accounts of early settlers, of Sir Wilfred Grenfell's medical mission, and the Hubbard expedition.

That evening I had the awkward feeling that we couldn't rid ourselves of Mark. *Did Ian tell him about our home, the bus?* Over breakfast the following morning I asked, "What if Mark follows us to the bus?"

"He won't."

"I hope you're right."

As expected, Mark found us again the following morning. How could he have missed us? There weren't many cars traveling south of Labrador City. The road back to Baie-Comeau seemed friendlier during daytime. By then we were used to the gravel, the dust, and roller-coaster peaks. And we didn't mind the frequent passes across railroad tracks. The wide taiga, the giant dams, iron ore mines, trucks with dynamite, an entire town under one roof! We thought we'd seen it all. Then we encountered scruffy-looking, bearded Joe, outside his decrepit pick-up truck on a turn-out by the road. I, always suspicious, urged Ian to drive on. But always the Good Samaritan, Ian stopped and asked if he needed help. Mark and I used the break to step out of the car and stretch. Joe, that's what he said his name was, told Ian that he didn't need help. He was just taking a break. But Ian, always ready to befriend anyone, engaged Joe in conversation. While they were talking, I heard a noise from Joe's vehicle. A child? Animal? I walked toward the truck, with Mark behind me. We peaked through the passenger window. *A rooster in the passenger seat? Who is this character traveling with a rooster?* Then I overheard what Joe was telling Ian.

"I'm driving back to Maine. I'm from there, you know. Make the trip every two years."

Ian asked what brought him to Labrador.

"Divorce. Nasty business. Had to move to an island here. Live off the land."

By then Joe had my curiosity. "Is the rooster going back to Maine?"

"Yeah. He's my best friend and companion."

"I'm getting a chicken," Ian said, and watched for my reaction.

"Then you'll be driving Miss Henrietta Cluck instead of Miss Daisy."

"Who's Miss Daisy?" Mark asked.

Joe looked puzzled but didn't say anything.

"Way too complicated," Ian said, "Time to move on. We have a ferry to catch."

On the ferry boat leaving Baie-Comeau, I thought about the strange places we'd seen and the people we met on the road to Labrador. I ended up liking Mark. At the ferry terminal we parted ways and never again saw him. Crossing the St. Laurence River I asked Ian if he thought the road to Goose Bay was worth the trip. He thought so. "What about you?"

"Absolutely. What impressed you the most?"

Ian said the iron ore mine was definitely a highlight, and the giant dam, then added that he relished the change of scenery between coniferous forests, bogs and lakes. He did regret not getting a tour of Churchill Fall's power plant but was pleased to have seen the amazing falls instead. The road had also impressed him, and the men who worked the motor graders; but he couldn't fathom that each worker lived in a small camper for weeks at a time to maintain a designated section of the road.

"There's a job for you if we ever give up the bus."

"You would miss me."

"You think so?" I said with a smile.

The drive to Goose Bay had been a voyage of exploration, the two of us venturing into the unknown. Alone in the dark, away from civilization, we watched the Aurora Borealis. We admired the unspoiled beauty of the land. I awaited more places on the North American continent to indulge our sense of adventure.

Geography of Quebec

A woman who cuts her hair is about to change her life.
Coco Chanel

In September 1999, my dilemma was to keep coloring my hair or to go natural. Unfortunately, I couldn't predict the natural shade. For years my hair had been dyed, highlights first, followed by full color that ranged from blonde to brown. A habit, not a need to appear younger. Yet now, three months into our trip, my shoulder length hair exposed an inch of grayish white roots. I didn't like the looks of it. Ian commented that I had snow on my roof and suggested I find a beauty parlor. I reminded him of my last appointment at the Beauty Institute in the morgue. Ian grinned and asked if I thought the mortician's services included hair coloring.

His remark made me giggle. "Wouldn't have surprised me." Then, with a more serious tone, I added that I wouldn't trust just any hairdresser.

"Don't be ridiculous," Ian said, "They're all the same."

"You're wrong." He couldn't understand the way women obsess over their hair, and that included me.

He asked what I wanted. To travel back to Florida every month? "Of course not." I knew that was out of the question. Still, what to do?

After leaving Labrador we'd driven along the St. Laurence River to Quebec City, then hurried on to Toronto. Ian had plans to join former business friends for a week of fishing at a lodge near North Bay, an annual event he'd attended for years. I opted to take a flight to New York City and visit Natasha. The day before my departure I looked in the mirror and from every angle, I inspected the colorless roots on my scalp. Was there more gray than white? At the normal rate of hair growth, a quarter of an inch per month, it would take almost two years for my color to grow out. In the interim, a white fuzzy crown would frame my face like the head of a Capuchin monkey. The only acceptable solution was to cut off my hair. I was fifty-four years old and ready for a change. Would I dare?

The day I went for my haircut in mid-town Manhattan I'd made up my mind. Natasha had highly recommended the salon. A young woman offered tea or coffee. Did I want a massage? I said that wasn't necessary. Just a haircut, wash and dry. She guided me to a basin. The shampoo seemed wasted on hair that was about to be discarded. Yet I savored the rich aroma of jasmine and roses.

"Conditioner?" she asked.

"No, thank you." I didn't bother to explain the futility of it.

With a towel wrapped turban-style around my head, I let her guide me to a chair in the styling area There I met Chris, a young man in his twenties. His short blond hair was in tiny spikes, a small gold earring in one ear. After the usual pleasantries, he ran his fingers through strands of my hair, looked at my profile in the mirror, asked what he could do for me.

"I'd like you to cut my hair off."

"How much would you like me to cut?"

"All of it. To the gray roots."

Chris looked startled and asked if I was sure. I told him yes.

"One hundred percent sure?"

"Absolutely."

Chris tried to talk me out of it, that I shouldn't go gray at my age.

Did I realize how long it would take to grow my hair back? I assured him that I'd thought about it, even calculated the time. He cut only a few inches to begin with, then swiveled the chair so I could see the result in the mirror. "You can change your mind."

"It's a page boy from the sixties."

"Looks good on you," Chris said.

I didn't tell him that when I started flying, Pan American had imposed that cut on all stewardesses. Hair wasn't allowed below the jaw line. I didn't like it then. "Keep cutting," I said firmly.

Dark strands fell to the floor. Chris took his time. He asked where I lived. I told him on a bus, and that my husband and I were permanent travelers without a home.

"No way!" Chris said.

I told him our bus was currently in Toronto, that I'd flown to New York City to visit my daughter, that we planned to zigzag across the North American continent and the following summer travel way up north into western Canada. Chris listened and kept snipping until I sensed his scissors close to my scalp.

"Are you ready?" Chris asked and, without waiting for my answer, turned the chair around.

Every bit of color was gone. I noticed shades of gray, whiter around my face, darker toward the back.

"I love it," I said. My head felt lighter. No more worries about hair falling in my face, a nuisance I'd fought for years. "Could you show me how to form spikes, like the ones you have?"

Chris rubbed gel between his thumb and fingers, then twisted small strands of hair into tiny points. I thanked him for a great job. He wished me luck with my travels. I hadn't asked about the cost of a cut when I made the appointment. The bill, one hundred eighty dollars, came as a surprise, a steep fee for what I considered a prisoner's haircut. Then I thought of all the money I would save by never coloring again.

Later that day, when Natasha saw me, she seemed pleased, said that I looked funky with my spiked head. My girlfriend in Manhattan was too polite to say anything, although I could tell she was shocked. Another friend tried to be diplomatic and told me that a pretty face can get away with anything. A few months later, Alec wasn't that kind. He took one look and said, "Mom, you're not going to stay like this." Back in Toronto Ian was waiting in the arrival hall and exclaimed, "What happened to you?" He placed emphasis on you, as if I had gotten into some sort of trouble.

"Don't you like my new hairdo?"

Ian shook his head. I told him that he would have to get used to it. Ian didn't mention my haircut again, but sometimes he called me a gray old lady. I didn't care. It took a year for my hair to grow a few inches. In the fall of 2000 in Oregon, I visited a hair salon and returned home with choppy strands of hair flipped up in the back. Ian had a name for it. "Well, look at the tufted titmouse," he said.

"Is that good or bad?" I asked, wondering where he came up with such remarks.

Ian meant he liked it, and I never colored my hair again.

If everything on earth were rational, nothing would happen.
Fyodor Dostoyevsky

"These came for you," said the owner of the West Memphis RV park, and pointed to eight boxes stacked against the wall in his office. Big lettering marked each one: *Property of the U.S. Government, Confidential.* I could tell the man was baffled by the way his gaze went back and forth, from the boxes to us.

"Who are you? Spies?"

For once Ian seemed stuck for words. We'd returned from a day's outing and were surprised at what we saw. Though we'd expected the material, we didn't foresee the quantity. And we never thought it would be officially labeled. Finally, to appease the man, Ian told him that we were on a secret mission about which we could not talk.

"Secret. I like that," the owner said, and offered to help transport the boxes to our bus. Five fit in the back of our Jeep Grand Cherokee. Our helper brought the remaining ones on his tractor. I had the feeling that he was thrilled to play a small part in our *secret mission*. Or maybe he wanted an excuse to see the interior of our vehicle. One by one we carried the boxes inside.

"Nice place," he commented. "Now tell me, who are you really?"

"Just a retired couple enjoying the country," Ian said, "Miss Daisy and I."

"You can't tell me that you're just some regular old folks traveling around in a fancy RV like that."

Ian shrugged his shoulders and smiled. I understood the man's suspicion. It was the middle of November, the end of the travel season. We were only one of three vehicles in the lot next to the muddy Mississippi. Of course, he wondered about the contents of the boxes. Before he could ask any more questions, Ian thanked him for his help and said we would be leaving early the following morning.

As soon as the owner stepped outside, we opened one of the boxes. It was stuffed with court documents. A second box contained files written in Korean.

"Why did they send me these?" Ian asked. "I can't read that."

I could see he was annoyed. Neither of us had anticipated the full scale of the project. Ian said it would require weeks to study the material. So much for retirement and travel, I thought. But Ian had signed a contract. Regardless of how time-consuming the work would be, it had to be completed.

Two weeks earlier, traveling on Interstate-75 between Atlanta and Chattanooga, our cell phone rang.

"Who is it?" Ian asked.

"Not sure. The Caller ID says U.S. Government."

"Answer it."

The caller identified himself as a lawyer for the Department of Justice and asked for Captain Duncan. I told Ian it was the Department of Justice.

"Tell them I'm driving on a busy interstate and can't talk until I get off. Tell them to call back in fifteen minutes."

As soon as I'd hung up, I asked Ian what he thought they wanted.

"No idea. Are you sure we paid all taxes."

Half an hour later we knew the nature of the call. The Department of Justice wanted Ian to be an expert witness for court proceedings that pertained to the Korean airline's Boeing 747 that crashed in Guam in 1997. I was curious how they found us. Ian told me that the lawyer, puzzled by the fact that we had no permanent home and traveled around the country in an RV, had received our contact information from a friend at the Flight Safety Foundation in Washington, D.C. where Ian was a committee member. If interested, Ian was to meet the lawyer and discuss the terms of the assignment. I encouraged Ian to go. We had the time and weren't in a hurry to be anywhere right then. Ian took a flight out of Chattanooga to Washington, D.C., and signed the contract. He would be well-compensated for studying the material, appearing in court, and writing an opinion, which had to be on the lawyer's desk no later than the 13th of December. When asked where to send the court documents, Ian gave the address of an RV park in West Memphis. He figured we would be there soon.

Now, two weeks later in West Memphis, we tried to find room for the boxes.

"Let's open them all up and see what's inside," I suggested. "Store the Korean ones."

Unfortunately the files were not in the order I'd expected. In fact, there was no particular order. We opted to keep one box in the living room and place the others in the cargo area, then switch them one by one. There was time. We had almost a month to complete the project. It was only the 17th of November.

The following morning, the RV park's owner and his wife watched us driving off, undoubtedly still questioning our secret mission. We traveled west to Arkansas. The Ouachita Mountains and Mount Magazine offered superb panoramas of meadows and forests. Unfortunately, the amount of trash, left to rot on private properties, reduced the appeal. We had a picnic at Haw Creek in the Ozark Forest. The weather was unusually mild for late November. I lay on the warm surface of a flat rock, enjoying the afternoon sun. The creek's water rippled behind me. A few birds rustled through the foliage on the ground. Ian, at a picnic table, was reading some of the documents. I'd closed my eyes and thought how quickly the past months had gone by.

The end of September, while still in Canada, we'd stumbled on the G.B. Shaw festival in Niagara-on-the-Lake and attended a few theatrical performances. And before returning to the United States, we enjoyed a picnic under an old oak tree at Ryerson Park on Lake Ontario. Was it in Northern Virginia or Maryland when I'd urged Ian to stop the bus on a country road so I could jump over a fence and pick apples? I couldn't remember the location, but recalled how Ian scolded me for being a thief. He'd been sure I would be arrested. Yet like a youngster stealing fruit from a neighbor's yard, I didn't think much of it. Slightly tart, crisp, and juicy, the apples were worth the trouble. My thoughts drifted to the late October foliage in the Great Smoky Mountains and how I climbed steps all alone to Mingo Falls in the Cherokee Reservation and admired the fine flow of water that resembled a veil over the rocky chasm. Life was peaceful then.

But more recently, while approaching Nashville, there'd been our heated dispute over navigation on I-40. I'd directed Ian to take the next exit east, as recommended in the campground directory. *Bullshit*, was his answer. He continued driving west. I'd said to do it his way, threw the map on the floor, and went to the bedroom. Ian ended up lost in downtown Nashville. After that fiasco, we'd agreed to navigational briefings before each departure.

A few days later we were in Oklahoma for Thanksgiving. The lawyer from the Department of Justice called Ian to notify him about a deposition in Los Angeles on December 6th. Where do you think we'll be by then, Ian wanted to know?

I looked over a map. "How about Albuquerque?"

We planned to spend a few days in Texas with Ian's oldest son, David. From there, the drive would take two days, not more. Ian called our travel agent in Miami and had her book a flight the afternoon of December 5th from Albuquerque to Los Angeles. It seemed like a perfect plan.

Success is not final, failure is not fatal: it is the courage
to continue that counts.
Winston Churchill

On December 4th we departed Fort Worth at 7 a.m. and stopped for gas not far out of town. At the cashier's inside the building, I overheard two truckers talking about the forecast of snow. Had I heard right? For the past days, it had been warm enough for a swim and sunbathing.

"Are you saying that we'll get snow?" I asked.

One of the men said there would be snow in Amarillo later that day. Back in the bus I told Ian what I'd heard.

"Snow? They're crazy. It's 70 degrees outside."

We drove off. Beside him, I studied the map. We opted to take route 287 via Wichita Falls to Amarillo, hoping to reach the border of New Mexico before day's end and spend the night. From there it was a short distance to Albuquerque for Ian's afternoon flight. I planned to take him to the airport, then return to the bus for a quiet evening alone, maybe stop at Blockbuster and rent a foreign movie.

Traffic was light that morning, the scenery monotonous. Ian wondered about his next meal and asked what I proposed for brunch. I suggested a Spanish omelet. He seemed pleased with the choice and agreed to stop somewhere before noon. At 10 a.m., west of Wichita

Falls, the first snowflakes appeared. I told Ian that I didn't like the looks of it. But he tried to reassure me. "The snow won't stick. The ground's too warm."

I didn't believe him. For the following thirty minutes I alternated between staring at the road ahead and watching the outside temperature fall on a gauge above the windshield. "Almost near freezing," I said, and reminded Ian that he'd promised months ago to park the bus if we encountered snow. By 11a.m. the flurries intensified, reducing visibility and, contrary to Ian's prediction, the snow stuck to the ground.

"All right I'll stop." Ian pulled to the side of the road, convinced that the storm would pass. "We'll eat something and wait for a snow plow to clear the road."

By then I'd lost my appetite for a Spanish omelet. Ian ate a sandwich. I watched big snowflakes stick to the windows. It wasn't long before snow covered the road. Ian looked fidgety.

"We can't stay here," he said and moved to the driver's seat. "How many miles to Amarillo?"

"About 180. All countryside. No big towns."

"Never mind. I'm going."

Just then a snow plow appeared, followed by a state police car. Not wasting any time, Ian pulled out behind them and followed in their tracks. I was horrified. Snow was piling up left and right. Except for the red and blue flashing lights of the police vehicle, visibility was reduced to a white blur. Here and there we passed a car stuck in a snow drift. Ian kept up with the patrol car ahead of us. I held tightly to the armrests as if that guaranteed safety. For fear of disturbing Ian, I didn't speak a word. Would we be the next casualty by the roadside in this isolated part of Texas? I pushed the thought away and reminded myself that I'd always trusted Ian's ability to fly airplanes in all types of weather. Innumerable people had relied on him to get them safely to their destination. He should be able to keep our vehicle on the road. One hour passed. Neither of us spoke. At one point I'd reached for my camera and focused on the patrol car ahead.

A photo for posterity in case we survived. Memories of my airline days came to mind. Severe in-flight turbulence and aborted landings during low visibility approaches hadn't frightened me. But that was years ago when I'd chosen the life of a stewardess. I hadn't chosen to drive our home through a blizzard. Once again I glanced at the map, wondering how much longer this ordeal would last. Shortly after one o'clock we passed a sign announcing Memphis. Were there many more places called Memphis in the USA?

"Maybe we should stay here."

"And do what?" Ian wanted to know.

Led by the snow plow and the police car, we passed through the small community, its buildings shrouded in snow flurries. Again Ian asked me how much longer it was to Amarillo. At the rate we were going, I told him at least another three hours. The snow plow and police car pulled off into a rest area. We drove on alone. Snowbanks on either side ruled out any possibility to stop and park. Neither Ian or I dared say a word for fear it might add to the tension. The bus moved forward in slow motion at 20 miles per hour. Time seemed to stand still until 3 p.m. on the outskirts of Claude, a small hamlet east of Amarillo. A large red and white neon-lit sign advertised The Goodnight Motel, rooms for $24.95, TV, local calls included.

"Hold on, I'm pulling into the parking lot," Ian said and stopped in front of the motel.

He gave the motel's owner twenty dollars for permission to stay and wait out the storm. Relieved to be off the road, I didn't care where we parked, lowered all the window shades, closed the curtains, and made tea.

"Might as well read some of the court files," I said. Ian was not keen on the idea but knew it had to be done. The report was due in nine days. By six o'clock we'd read through a pile of folders and made notes. I raised one of the shades to peek outside. Darkness had set in. The snow hadn't stopped. Heavy flakes whirled around the neon-lit motel sign.

"Looks like we're spending the night here. How about some light dinner?"

"What do we have?"

"Left-over stuffed peppers."

I heated them in the microwave, added some French bread from the freezer. Exhausted from the day's events, we soon went to bed. Ian fell asleep immediately. I was too keyed up. The idea of sleeping in a parking lot in some strange place in Texas troubled me. I kept hearing the grating of snow plows. Several loud whistles announced the passage of a nearby train. Sleep eventually came. Then the rumbling noise of the bus's engine awakened me. Half asleep I reached for Ian. He was not in bed. The clock showed 2 a.m. I peeked out the window. The snow had stopped. I heard Ian's voice from up front telling me we were moving on.

I called out, "You've got to be kidding. At this time of night?"

"Gotta be in Albuquerque by noon."

I didn't understand the rush. Albuquerque was only four hours from Amarillo by interstate. I mumbled words of protest, got dressed, and told him I was ready. But the bus didn't move. I heard the engine shutting off, then restarting, and enquired about the problem.

"The damn thing doesn't want to go in gear. You try it. Maybe you have the magic touch."

For the first time since we'd bought the bus, I sat in the driver's seat.

"What do I do?"

"Turn on the engine," Ian said, and showed me how to place the key. The engine started. I pushed the gear buttons. Nothing.

I got up. "You should never have driven in snow."

That's the last thing Ian wanted to hear. He told me to shut up, grabbed his flashlight, and went outside. A minute later he was back. "The damn bus is covered with ice." He didn't know what to do about the gear issue and suggested we drive the car to town, locate a phone booth, and call a repair shop and towing company. As usual our cell phone was useless.

"It's Sunday morning," I said. "Who do you think is awake at 3 a.m.

to answer your call?"

Ian didn't respond and went to unhook the car. It was fifteen degrees outside. Bundled in winter clothes, we drove the short distance to downtown Claude where the only phone booth in town was outside a coffee shop adjacent to a Texaco gas station. Eighteen-wheelers were parked left and right, their drivers forming a long line in front of the booth. Ian suggested we take turns standing in line. He waited first. I stepped inside the coffee shop. Truckers occupied every table. I heard their loud, frustrating comments about the weather. Some with extra cash in hand were playing the gambling machines by the wall. It took over an hour for Ian to get to the phone booth. Unable to reach the repair service or the towing company, he vented his frustration with a truck driver who suggested using cardboard to cover the intake and exhaust airflow to the engine compartment. Before returning to the bus Ian thought we might be in need of extra cash and tried to locate a bank. The only one in town did not have an ATM.

Back at the bus, Ian wedged cardboard between louvers on the engine's air inlet and exit. By eight o'clock the sun had come up. I noticed how shabby the motel looked. Rust colored paint was chipping off its doors and windows. I counted ten rooms with pick-up trucks in front. Piles of snow lined the road and parking lot. The sky had turned a cloudless bright blue. *If only we'd waited a day*. An hour passed. The bus refused to move. So much for the cardboard, I thought. As the morning progressed, the temperature rose above freezing, and the ground surrounding the bus turned to a slushy, yellow muck, which stuck to Ian's boots and made its way inside. Before long our light blue carpet was smudged with it, and a putrid odor penetrated our living area. Somewhere I'd read Amarillo got its name because of the yellow soil. I didn't know it stank. I suggested that Ian take off his boots before entering the bus.

He snapped, "I've bigger worries than a dirty carpet."

By eleven o'clock we knew Ian would be unable to make his flight out of Albuquerque. Back to the phone booth, this time to contact our travel agent. Luckily we had her home number. She rebooked Ian out of Amarillo. And on the phone, an agent from the towing company promised Ian that a truck was on the way. But no-one appeared by four in the afternoon. When Ian returned once again from the phone booth, he looked exasperated. Out of breath and close to tears, he sat bent over on the sofa. "The tow trucks are told to clear the interstate before getting to us."

"What does that mean?"

"We won't see one before tomorrow." Ian told me to pack, that we were driving to Amarillo to get a hotel.

"What about the bus?"

"Obviously it stays here."

Great, I thought, he will leave me to deal with the mess. We hurried to pack a few clothes, locked the bus, drove to Amarillo, and checked into a Marriott at the airport.

The following morning, Ian's flight left at 7:30. I returned to the bus and waited for the tow truck, which didn't arrive until noon. The driver, a tall lanky fellow, took a few slow strides around the bus, briefly peeked under its belly, then asked if I knew how to drive it. I said I didn't. But he insisted.

"You could drive with the shift in neutral and steer it behind the tow vehicle."

"I cannot do that," I said firmly. "My husband is in charge of driving. He's not here." I took my handbag, sat in the car, and watched him hook the bus to the truck. I didn't know then that he was supposed to disconnect the drive shaft to the axles, a messy task that required him to get underneath the vehicle. His refusal to do so caused another malfunction later on.

Once the bus was on its way to the transmission shop, I drove through Amarillo, had lunch, and returned to the hotel for the evening. The repair was simple. Due to the ice and snow, a bundle of wires had broken off underneath. The following morning a mechanic at the repair shop was kind enough to drive the bus to an RV park. I rented a Rug Doctor and spent a few hours shampooing the carpet, restoring its original color. By the time Ian returned from Los Angeles that evening, our home looked and smelled clean. Yet I didn't let him forget how much I resented his decision to drive through a blizzard and made him promise to never again put me through such an ordeal. His promise lasted only a little over a year.

On December 8th, we continued on to Albuquerque. The plateau of New Mexico was a welcome sight: its mesas and open prairies, its landscape with limestone formations and short bushy vegetation, the antelopes grazing in fields. Long freight trains with multi-colored containers moved on tracks parallel to the interstate. The RV park at Kirtland Air Force Base in Albuquerque became our new location. At the commissary we bought frozen meals and cold cuts for sandwiches. We planned to stay inside the bus for the following days to finalize the report, which had to be faxed before midnight eastern standard time on December 13th to the Department of Justice.

Arguments are to be avoided.
They are always vulgar and often convincing.
Oscar Wilde

Ian and I should have anticipated the stress of working together for five long days within the confines of the bus. We'd already failed in the kitchen and were incapable of preparing a meal together. The two of us *could spoil the broth*, as the saying goes. Still, that week in December 1999 we had good intentions. I expected Ian to tell me what to write. He expected me to give his words a logical structure. A simple, combined effort, we thought. Instead, the task became a test of our marriage. As the days progressed and the deadline loomed, tensions escalated.

The first day we set out to work after breakfast. Window shades down and snap-on blinds inside the windshield meant total privacy as we organized the documents according to historical events, previous accidents, interviews with the airline's employees, and FAA findings. By afternoon, stacks of folders with yellow sticky notes were on every flat surface. By the end of that day more were piled on the floor and eventually on our bed. We worked into the night, ate a quick meal, and slept.

On the second morning, I suggested fresh air and a short walk before we started but Ian wanted to stay inside and watch the morning news. I ventured out into the 18 degree weather. The small RV lot held four other vehicles. Not a person around. I didn't stay out long, felt chilled, and fatigued from the 4000 feet altitude. Ian's head was bent over documents on the dining table. "Get the computer. I'm ready to dictate."

"No breakfast?"

"Not hungry."

If Ian had no appetite, he was anxious. Not a good omen. I sat on one of the couches and opened the laptop. I'd barely finished one page before the first argument erupted. I said he was speaking too fast.

"Don't interrupt me!"

"Slow down. I can't type that quickly." I wasn't a good typist, but faster than Ian who used his right index finger. I asked him to repeat what he'd said.

Ian wanted to know where we were. I read the last sentence. But he kept skipping from one topic to another. "You're confusing me. Focus on one finding at a time."

"Write. You can organize it later."

Ian's impatience made me nervous. And in trying to correct his wording, I fell behind again. "Wait. You're not finishing a sentence."

"For God's sake, just write."

I didn't like his authoritative tone. "Write it yourself." I closed the laptop and placed it in front of him.

Ian said nothing. Back on the couch, I raised the shades and stared out the window. Without foliage the honey locust looked bleak. Fifteen minutes passed.

"Are you going to pout all day?"

"Yes, unless you change your tone."

He handed the laptop back. Again I copied down the information he'd gathered. And except for a brief break for lunch we worked all-day. I printed the pages.

By the third morning we looked disheveled. Ian hadn't taken a shower. After days of not shaving, gray stubble covered his chin. I'd foregone the use of make-up. And my grizzled hair looked like a badly thatched roof. Ian suggested we get the ordeal over with and write the initial draft. By then he'd formed an outline of the report in his mind. I sat down, ready to type. During his career Ian had dictated to a secretary who typed letters and documents without questioning the contents. But I didn't see myself as his secretary. I had my own ideas for the report and, with my knowledge of airline operations, tried to evaluate Ian's findings. What I deemed inconsequential and meaningless I refused to include. At one point I stopped typing. "You cannot say that."

Ian admonished me. I was interrupting his train of thought.

"What you're saying doesn't make sense."

"Just write."

"You don't understand. You need references to support your thoughts."

"Why don't you shut up?"

"Stop yelling."

Our voices reached a crescendo that ended in screaming.

"I'll get someone else to write it."

"Be my guest."

I had to overcome my desire to throw the laptop somewhere. Instead I put it down, paced the hallway, and went to the bedroom. In the living room the TV came on. Thoughts went through my mind. Why does Ian have to be so difficult? What happened to the intimate togetherness Ian advocated when he talked me into this life on the bus? And now, I'm doing him a favor. He cannot write the document by himself. Why can't we work as a team? An hour later, I craved a cup of tea and went to the kitchen. Ian had an exasperated look on his face. I heard him mumble that our working together was a big mistake. He should never have agreed to it. I said that it was too late to change things. The work had to be done, whether we liked it or not. I felt partly responsible for encouraging him to accept the job. A cup of tea and a few cookies later, we continued.

On day four, I saw no reason to dress and stayed in pajamas. I wasn't going out. Ian had gotten up before me that morning. When I saw him, he looked withdrawn. I tried to make conversation but received only one-word answers. I'd seen him in such a state before, on days prior to his annual check-rides at Pan American. Stress from striving for perfection. I'd learned to leave him alone during those times. Now I couldn't.

"We need to get going on this," I said, emphasizing we.

He agreed. Hours went by without drama. A miracle I thought. Yet before the day was over, we clashed over bullets, paragraphs, and indents. Ian didn't understand me because he wasn't in front of the computer screen. As if I were speaking a foreign language, my words didn't register. And his impatience put me in a frenzy.

"You don't understand the computer."

"You don't either."

"I know more than you do."

"You think you do," Ian yelled and threw his notepad on the floor.

"I can't do what you're asking me. I quit!"

Sensing the urge to get away, I put a coat over my pajamas and went outside. The late afternoon sun illuminated the snowcapped Sandia Mountains with an amber glow. The scenery, so magnificent, deserved a photo. I retrieved my camera which I kept in a drawer behind the driver's seat of the bus.

"Back so soon?" Ian asked.

I didn't look at him but could imagine his sheepish grin.

"Not to see you." Camera in hand, I stepped out again.

After I'd taken a few pictures, I considered going for a drive through Albuquerque? But that required getting dressed. I went back inside.

"Sorry I yelled at you," Ian said.

"You drive me nuts." I said that I was on strike but might change my mind with an increase in pay.

"Write yourself a check."

"I will. So, where were we....?"

That night, I printed for the first time, all twenty pages of the report.

On the fifth day, December 13th, the report had to be faxed by 10 p.m. Today it would be sent via email. Not in 1999, when my Internet options were a slow land line in a library or a phone booth. With last minute changes Ian took his time. We didn't take a break to eat. I printed the document four more times.

At six o'clock Ian asked, "How long do you think Kinko's stays open?"

I called the store to make sure they stayed open late. Shortly before nine I printed the final version, put it in a folder, and rushed out to the car. Kinko's was twenty minutes away. The report was faxed just before the deadline. Back home I opened a bottle of wine. I didn't know yet that my work wasn't over.

Early the following morning we left the bus at the Detroit Diesel Service Center in town. Besides an oil change, the transmission seal needed replacing. Ever since the tow truck driver in Amarillo hadn't disconnected the drive shaft, the seal leaked. We were in the car on our way to brunch when the cellphone rang.

"It's the Department of Justice," I told Ian.

He stopped the car, spoke briefly, and said, "There's a problem."

"They don't like the report?"

"We have to change some of the wording."

"That's no problem."

"But it must be done within three hours."

We rushed back to the service center and told the manager we needed to get inside our vehicle.

"Impossible," he said, "Customers aren't allowed in the work area."

Our home occupied one of the many vehicle bays in an enormous enclosed garage. Ian pleaded. We had to get to our computer and printer to finish an important project for the U.S. government. There was a deadline. People's lives depended on our work. The Service Manager shook his head. A bus, governmental work? People's lives depended on an older couple in a bus? I don't know what made him change his mind, but he agreed to make an exception. Maybe he thought we were running from the law and could endanger his facility. He said we could retrieve what we needed from the bus and do the work in the customer waiting area. He pointed to a corner behind us. I looked back and saw a coffee table loaded with outdated magazines, four chairs against the wall, the carpet in need of cleaning. Ian and I hurried to the bus, grabbed what we needed, returned to the waiting area. By then the chairs were taken. I looked for a wall outlet to plug in the printer, then sat on the floor, my back resting against the wall. The work took longer than I'd anticipated. Customers walked in and out. I had the weird sensation that all eyes were on me. One person almost stumbled over my feet. Ian explained that I was homeless and needed to do homework for school. I nodded my head as if it were true. *Would anyone believe the truth?*

The printer spit out the new version. We gathered our equipment and hurried back to Kinko's. The lawyer called, was pleased with the changes, and told Ian about a court date in early January. That evening we celebrated by going out for dinner and congratulated each other on a job well done.

Nobody is walking out on this fun, old-fashioned family Christmas.
Clark Griswold, National Lampoon Christmas

Our first holiday season on the road should be named the *Duncan National Lampoon's Christmas on the Bus*. Alec and Natasha were coming home. Eager to share life on the bus with them, we looked forward to the reunion. I hoped to re-create the festive celebration of years past with our usual gift exchange on Christmas Eve. A fairy-tale event, the way I remembered it when our children were little. In anticipation of their arrival, Ian and I made space in closets and

took several containers with summer clothes and unessential equipment to a rented storage unit. I bought a small Christmas tree, pre-decorated with ornaments. Outside, below the windshield, we hung a wreath of fir evergreens with red ribbons. And to re-assure our friends that we were still a couple seven months into our journey, we sent out a Christmas card that showed Ian in a Santa costume and me dressed as his elf, standing by the front door of our home.

Alec arrived first at the Albuquerque airport on December 17th. I knew he would have preferred to spend the holiday in Coral Gables, his home for five years before college. How would he share such limited space with his nineteen-year-old sister? The living room couches made into beds, one a full size, the other a single. I thought he and Natasha could flip coins for the bigger couch. A day later, Natasha arrived from New York. I'd told both kids to pack lightly. Natasha came with an oversized suitcase and an evening gown. And when she lost the coin flip, she pouted. I'd seen that face before. Why does he always get the better deal? I remembered the old sibling rivalry only too well and suggested they could switch beds after a few days.

Ian and I hadn't seen much of Albuquerque. The four of us visited the Atomic Bomb Museum, strolled around the Old Town, and went out for dinner. That night, after Ian and I retired to bed, Alec drove Natasha to the crest of the Sandia Mountains, 10,600 feet high. When Ian heard about their escapade he scolded Alec.

"That's not a road to drive in the dark."

"But you should have seen the view," Natasha's eyes lit up while she described the panorama of the city's shimmering lights.

I preferred not to think about what could have happened.

A day later, Ian planned to leave for Santa Fe at an early hour. Early to Ian meant by nine o'clock. Early to our children meant not before ten, preferably after eleven. We were sitting in bed, having coffee at eight that morning when Ian thought it was time for the kids to wake up.

"Rise and shine," I hollered, hoping for a reaction. Nothing. I walked up front. The pulled out beds took the entire living area. Both of them were sound asleep, their clothes and bags spread over the dining table. With a gentle mother's touch I nudged them.

"Time to get up."

Natasha pulled the covers over her head. Alec groaned. Ian was getting impatient. The beds blocked his passage to the front door. He told me to get the kids moving. I glanced briefly out the window. Snowflakes whirled around the bus, the temperature below freezing. Not again, I thought, and suggested we wait. Why not get to Santa Fe a day later? Ian was undeterred and said, as long as we left within the hour we'd be fine.

This time I jostled my sleeping beauties. "Get up! It's going to snow."

Alec was the first one dressed and went outside to help his father. Natasha protested but helped me clear away the clutter. She hadn't given any thought to the reality that everything on the vehicle needed storing before we drove off. With each one of us feeling the need to rush, moods soured. So much for a happy holiday, I thought, and went out to hook up the car. Alec had already done so. My recollection of what happened next is blurry. Was I the culprit? Was it Alec? Somehow in the rush of getting things done we'd left the Jeep's gear shift in the wrong position. To tow it, the transmission had to be set to *park*, the transfer case to *neutral* in order for the wheels to turn. We drove off. Natasha went back to sleep. Alec sat in the passenger seat. At the dining table, I stared out the window. Visibility was poor, light snow falling. At least Santa Fe was only one and a half hours away.

Directions to the RV park in Santa Fe were unclear. Annoyed with the poor signs, Ian made a sharp turn into a large parking lot. And in his turn, he saw our car, its rear wheels dragging. I saw it, too and felt my heart sink. *My fault? I'm never going to hear the end of this*. Ian stormed out, unhooked the vehicle, and tried to drive it. The transmission was fried.

Natasha had woken up and asked, "Where are we?"

"In a parking lot at a correction facility," Alec answered.

"O joy!" Natasha said, "We're going to spend Christmas with convicts."

Just as she said this, two prison guards arrived in their patrol car. They told Ian he couldn't park there. Ian assured them we had no intention to spend the night and were waiting for a tow service. The guards said that it wouldn't have been the first time that people tried to overnight their RV.

We waited two hours for the car to be towed to a local dealership. Ian rented a cheap sedan, the type of car Alec considered below his standards. Worse, the rental contract forbade him to drive it. By the time we arrived at the RV park, a foul mood prevailed. I was depressed. Alec was furious because he couldn't drive the rental car. Natasha thought this bus life was awful and lamented that we'd sold our home. Ian was taking it better than all of us, considering the car needed a new transmission at the cost of several thousand dollars, and that it would be at least a week before the car was repaired. Before going to sleep that night, I prayed for better days ahead.

Overnight my disposition improved. Surely there was nothing to gain by brooding over my mistake. After a cup of coffee I went to brush my teeth and turned the faucet. No water came out. It can't be. I knew that we were hooked to the water line at the RV park. With my mouth full of toothpaste, I yelled, "Why is there no water?" I used a Kleenex to get the toothpaste off my face.

"I'll check," Ian said. But he couldn't get past the kids' beds. That's when the clutter got to him. I tried to calm him down and told him not to expect the same orderliness with four people on the bus. But Ian didn't see it that way. "This place is a pig's sty," he said and blamed Natasha for taking a twenty minute shower the night before. "You had to wash your damn hair and use all the hot water."

Natasha put a pillow over her head. She didn't want to hear the accusations. As we soon discovered, Natasha wasn't the culprit. An overnight temperature in the single digits had frozen the pipes under the bathroom. I tried to defrost them by holding a hair dryer under the sink. After an hour I gave up. We went out for breakfast and hoped the pipes would thaw as the day warmed.

That night we attended a concert of seasonal music at one of the oldest churches in Santa Fe. I hoped the Christmas spirit would reach us at last. But the seats I'd obtained earlier were not together. Two seats were on the left, two on the right of the nave. Ian and Alec didn't like the arrangement. "I don't want to be here" was written all over Alec's face. During the intermission Ian said that he hadn't liked the music and would, for that reason, not attend the second part. Natasha called them spoiled brats. Yet she was adamant to not let their behavior bother her, and told me to do the same.

On the 23rd of December the stars were better aligned. The kids and I looked forward to skiing. Alec and Natasha even managed to get out of bed before nine that morning. Ian was happy to stay home. As I drove the rental car up the mountain to *Ski Santa Fe*, I recalled the times when I'd taken both children out of school on Wednesday afternoons to Mohawk Mountain in Northwestern Connecticut where they'd grown up. Alec was six, Natasha four when they first learned to ski.

The lift took us to 11,000 feet. Snow dusted spruces lined the slopes. A natural Christmas wonderland, Natasha commented. Alec raced down the slopes. I marveled that he hadn't forgotten his technique. I remembered someone telling me that skiing is like bike riding. Once you know it, you never forget. As we drove home later that afternoon, the western sky turned reddish pink, the prairie below a glowing burnt-orange, and dark purple shaded the mountains. We stopped to take photos. *For purple mountain majesties above the fruited plain!* Natasha sang with the voice of a trained soprano. New Mexico was rightfully named the land of enchantment. We returned home happy.

As was our family tradition, we opened gifts the night before

Christmas. Even when the children were little, Santa came to our house the afternoon of Christmas Eve. He couldn't possibly visit all the houses in one night, I'd told them. We were going to keep the same tradition on the bus. For dinner I suggested a wide selection of delicacies, a gourmet Smorgasbord. We all ended up at the market. Ian wanted shrimp, Alec salmon, and Natasha craved French bread and paté. And we had to have cheeses and a few French pastries. The more we shopped, the hungrier we got, and the more we bought. Our twenty cubic foot refrigerator/freezer came in handy that day.

In the afternoon we toured the red and yellow limestone canyons of the Western Hills. Elk and mule deer grazed in an enormous caldera. Sadly, the pueblos I'd found so appealing forty years earlier now seemed run-down. Alec's highlight was driving by the Los Alamos National Laboratory. At six that evening I closed the shades in our living room and put on Christmas music. Natasha prepared platters with food and placed them on the bar. I opened a bottle of champagne. We'd dressed up and hoped to enjoy Christmas in style. Gifts wrapped with bows sat on the kitchen counter, the Christmas tree on a side table. Alec looked comfortable in the passenger chair, swiveled around and tilted in La-Z-Boy fashion. Natasha, Ian, and I sat on the couches. We exchanged gifts slowly. As is customary in our family, the recipient has to guess the contents of the package before untying the bow and ripping the paper. In the interim we enjoyed the smorgasbord. A perfect Christmas Eve, the distress of the past days forgotten. That's until we heard Natasha screaming for help from the bathroom at 10:30 p.m.

I hurried over to her. She was standing in water. The toilet had overflowed. I grabbed every reachable towel to mop the mess. Ian shouted that the tank must be full and went into a rage, blaming all of us. Alec, always quick to find a solution, reacted to Ian's outburst by putting on his coat and hat. He rushed outside to pull the handle that opens the valve on the waste water holding tank, which contains both gray water (shower and sink) and toilet waste. Usually, at an RV park, the waste hose is attached to the park's septic system. But it wasn't recommended that the valve stay open during an overnight freeze. Alec was unaware of that. All the waste from the holding tank gushed out. Alec was mortified. Ian went berserk. Natasha cried. My blood pressure went so high I decided to have a stiff drink. Thank goodness there was no other vehicle at the RV park. Why would anyone brave the cold winters in New Mexico? For the next hour and a half we took turns hosing the mess down a ravine. It was midnight when I went to bed. O holy night.

The next morning, Christmas Day, I wondered what else could go wrong. We finished breakfast and started a general clean-up. I was washing dishes when the water stopped. "No, not again."

"Don't blame me," Natasha responded. "I haven't taken a shower."

"I haven't either. This is unfair."

Ian thought our water tank was empty and instructed Alec to go out and fill it with fresh water from the RV park's system. Alec did as he was told. But as soon as he'd turned the water valve, the fitting burst, and beside the bus, a giant water fountain gushed 12 feet high. I saw the awful scene from the window and screamed, "Ian."

"Jesus," he yelled and hurried off to locate the RV park's owner. Alec came inside, and threw down his wet coat, gloves, and hat. Looking sad and frustrated, he asked, "Why are we doing this, Mom?"

"I didn't plan it this way."

Ian returned without having found the owner. What to do next? For a while we sat there stone-faced, sunk in our unhappiness. Outside the bus, gallons of water sprayed into the air. In an attempt to change the morose mood, I said, "Look at it this way. We've Old Faithful outside, just like being in Yellowstone."

Natasha didn't think it was funny. An hour later the owner came and turned off the main water valve to the RV park.

"Freezing temperatures cause this," he said. "Merry Christmas!"

"Bah Humbug," I responded.

By then all of us were ready to move to a hotel. Every towel was wet and dirty, clothes required washing, and we needed showers. To my surprise, the owner repaired the water pump connection in no time. I could do laundry. We took showers in the afternoon and went for a delightful New Mexican Christmas dinner at the Inn of the Azanazi, the best restaurant in town.

After another day of skiing it was time to move back to Albuquerque. Our car was still at the transmission repair shop in Santa Fe. And because the rental car wasn't equipped to be towed, I drove it behind the bus. In the early morning hours of December 29th our children left to fly home. I was sad to see them leave and passed the day cleaning and doing laundry, my remedy against sadness. I wished the visit had been less stressful. Maybe my expectations were too high. I went to sleep early with the hope that the negative memories would evaporate, so pleasant ones would prevail.

Ian and I chose to ring in the Millennium, the beginning of 2000, in our cozy bedroom, watching the televised festivities from around the world. Leading up to that night, the news covered worrywarts, who anticipated computers crashing, financial institutions failing, and plane travel being disrupted. Nothing happened. I wasn't sure if the naysayers were disappointed or relieved. We only hoped that the New Year would grant us a safe journey and continuing good health.

Health is not valued till sickness comes.
Thomas Fuller.

Early in January of 2000, the symptoms started one evening. Ian couldn't move his right arm without severe pain. Getting a shirt on or off was agonizing. Convinced that something was wrong with his shoulder, he looked in the Albuquerque *Yellow Pages* for an orthopedic surgeon. But an appointment wasn't easy. He heard, *We don't take new patients. You don't live here. We can't treat you.* Eventually Ian found a physician who saw him on short notice. An x-ray revealed nothing abnormal. But cortisone in the affected shoulder didn't bring relief. A week later the pain traveled to other parts of his body. Ian barely endured a bed sheet on his back. For hours he sat up in bed. I felt helpless. What could be the cause of his maladies? The orthopedic surgeon referred him to a rheumatologist.

The receptionist at the rheumatologist's office asked his address and phone number. Ian gave Alec's Daytona address and our cellphone number.

"How long will you be in Albuquerque?"

"A week, maybe longer."

"Where are you staying?"

"On a bus."

The receptionist wondered if she'd understood correctly. "Did you say bus?"

Ian confirmed she'd heard right.

"Few people are as nutty as we are," I added.

"Are you his wife?"

"No, that's Miss Daisy. I'm her driver."

I smiled, glad to see despite his ailment, Ian had not lost his sense of humor. The receptionist looked at me, then at Ian, shook her head, and said the doctor would see him shortly. In the waiting room, I whispered in Ian's ear that she probably thought we needed a psychiatrist. After a brief consultation, the rheumatologist prescribed prednisone. Ian was to return in two weeks. At the thought of having to remain longer in Albuquerque, Ian groaned. Although we liked the city's restaurants, art center and theater, we were eager to move on.

The prednisone worked a miracle. After two days Ian felt better. On January 26th he flew to Los Angeles for the deposition. On the 31st we celebrated my fifty-fifth birthday. The night before snow had fallen. I awakened to a beautiful wintry landscape. To pass the time until Ian's second appointment, we took daytrips. The scenery to Taos was spectacular. Yet I felt disappointed. The small artsy village I'd fallen in love with in the 1960s was now a tourist trap. Another excursion took us to the Plains of St. Augustine. Twenty-seven enormous radio telescopes sprouted like giant mushrooms in the deserted valley. Made famous by the movie *Contact*, this *Very Large Array* of radio telescopes (VLA) captures radio waves from space. The intent is to receive signals from another living planet in the billions of galaxies in the universe. Would the earth even exist, after the sound traveled thousands of light-years through space?

On February 11th, the rheumatologist had a diagnosis: lupus. What did he mean? Ian had never heard of lupus and asked, jokingly, if lupus was some sort of venereal disease. The doctor didn't appreciate the humor, said the illness was difficult to treat, ordered blood tests, and asked Ian to return in March. I knew lupus meant wolf in

Latin. What could Ian's pain possibly have to do with an animal? At the local library I searched the Internet for information. I learned that lupus refers to a facial rash that resembles a wolf's bite. Ian's face showed none of these characteristics.

The prognosis was upsetting. Our nomadic life could not include a major illness requiring treatments, follow-up visits, refills on prescriptions. Ian was adamant we not spend another month in Albuquerque. He wanted to be in Arizona in March, then head to Death Valley and California in April. If he needed to see the rheumatologist, we would park the bus, travel to Albuquerque by car, and stay in a motel.

The following morning we left. I'd fallen in love with New Mexico. The desert's soft rose colors, the clear, deep blue sky, the spectacular sunsets, rocky limestones, the valleys and basins. Sadly, this beauty of the countryside didn't translate to the villages. Adobe style homes blending with the landscape were a rarity. And the small towns were predictable. On the outskirts, a sales lot for domestic trailers, junkyards with scrapped old cars and discarded appliances. The centers of towns with a Walmart and chain restaurants. Even historic mining towns, so captivating in John Wayne's movies, lacked an allure of the Wild West. Yet the countryside still gave this impression. I could imagine a lone horseman advancing across the desert grassland, and Geronimo and his Apache band appearing on a clifftop. At White Sands National Monument, Ian and I sledded down gypsum dunes and admired the few resilient plants that had broken through the tough surface and survived despite the aridity.

And alone in the Gila Forest we encountered deer, foxes, and a mountain lion before reaching the Cliff Dwelling National Monument. In the 13th century, the 200 feet high dwellings of the Mogollon tribe contained fifty rooms to accommodate several families. A narrow path led from one alcove to the next. I clung to the wall, away from the precipice, and thought about the danger to children. How did Mogollon mothers prevent them from sliding off the cliff? Did they keep their children on ropes? A few days later on a path near Massai Point, 7000 feet high in Southern Arizona's Chiricahua National Monument, I carefully minded my own footing while admiring the landscape of sandstone spires and pinnacles.

Compared to New Mexico, dusty southern Arizona had less appeal. Ian predicted in the not too distant future the area would resemble the Sahara. People apparently liked spending winters in Arizona. Enormous RV parks were stuffed with hundreds of vehicles, and for those who failed to secure a reservation or preferred a less crowded environment, there was the desert. We passed by RVs and trailers parked randomly across the barren sand or along the Colorado River. They recalled the small gypsy colonies I'd seen in Europe. By St. Patrick's Day we reached Williams, a historic small town on the old Route 66, and the gateway to the Grand Canyon. There we stumbled on a local diner that offered the traditional Irish corned beef and cabbage.

I regretted not being able to walk along the Great Canyon as I'd done the summer of 1966. Together with other visitors, Ian and I had to board a shuttle bus that stopped at several lookout points. Yet, I felt the same awe as years before. Frosty patches of snow on the Western slopes glistened under the midday sun and added beauty to the terrain's majestic appeal. When we stopped at a Navajo Trading Post, I was tempted to purchase a rug or a piece of pottery as I had forty years earlier. The current prices changed my mind.

Back in the bus, facing a terrain inhabited by prairie dogs, we watched them chase each other while debating if Ian should keep his appointment with the rheumatologist. Was it worth a ten-hour roundtrip by car to Albuquerque? As always, Ian made the decision. A short side trip, he called it, and suggested we stop in Flagstaff at a mail facility and ship the documents back to the Department of Justice in Washington, D.C. In Albuquerque, the rheumatologist ordered more prednisone, and asked Ian to return in three months. We didn't. At the time, Ian wasn't aware of prednisone's long-term effects.

In Seattle six weeks later Ian went for a second opinion. This time, the doctor urged Ian to stop traveling, to remain in the city for five or six months, and to try different medications. Ian wouldn't hear of it. If we stayed in Seattle over the summer, we would have to postpone our travels to Western Canada and Alaska for an entire year. Instead, he asked for a new prescription of prednisone with several refills and said he would return in the fall. We didn't foresee the difficulty of receiving the medication. The mail-order pharmacy affiliated with Ian's retired military status could send pills only to our legal address in Daytona. Alec forwarded them via FedEx overnight delivery. But the farther north we traveled, an overnight service could mean several days. One package zigzagged for a week through Western Canada. After missing us in Fort Nelson, it went by truck 640 miles south-east to Edmonton, then by air to Vancouver. FedEx offered to dispatch it 1300 miles north to Watson Lake via a Greyhound bus, but could not guarantee the frequency of the bus service. The "overnight" package finally reached us in Whitehorse.

We were in Tok, Alaska, in early July when Ian was again out of pills. The mail had not reached us that Friday, and the local pharmacy, part of a small makeshift clinic, closed at noon. He'd been warned about stopping Prednisone abruptly and made an emergency call for the clinic to re-open so he could receive his medication. A year would pass before we stayed in one place long enough for treatment.

As inconceivable as it may seem when we took to the road, Ian and I had not considered the possibility of an illness. Years of good health had deluded us. Except for the occasional cold and flu, our primary reason to see a doctor was for routine physicals. Even Ian's recent hip replacement and a minor procedure on my knee failed to cause alarm. Despite our advanced ages, we considered ourselves young and fit, ignoring the reality of growing older and the inevitable physical problems. When we became nomads we had taken our good health for granted and focused on the journey and the adventure that awaited us.

Sometimes people don't want to hear the truth because
they don't want their illusion destroyed.
Friedrich Nietzsche

Our accountant suggested we form a corporation. In this way we could protect ourselves from liability and defer some income from Ian's consulting work. After retiring, Ian was with a team that conducted airline safety audits and therefore favored a corporation. I wasn't against the idea but wondered about a corporation on the bus. Ian called Alec in Daytona and asked him to look in the Yellow Pages for an attorney. Of the three names Alec provided, a woman named Melissa agreed to the task. She would file the documents with the state of Florida, which for tax purposes was still our state of residency, then apply for a tax ID number. Ian was pleased. A simple procedure and minimal expense.

We were in Tucson at the end of February when Melissa called and said the documents were ready to be signed and notarized. Could we come to her office? Ian thought she was joking. Could we receive a fax? Ian wasn't sure and asked me where we could locate a fax machine.

"Did you tell her we live on a bus?"

"No. Only that we were traveling."

"What about one of these mail places?" I'd seen one not too far away from where we were parked. I said to tell her we would call back with the number.

We drove to the place and alerted the business that we were expecting an important fax. By the time *Duncan Aviation Enterprises LLC* was formed, we were on a first name basis with every employee at *Mail Boxes Etc.*

After the corporation was filed and we had a tax ID number, we needed a business checking account. Our bank in Coral Gables, Florida, seemed the logical place to start. I called and was transferred to their business division, said my husband and I wanted to open a business checking account. The bank officer inquired about our business. Aviation consulting I told her.

"I can set up an appointment at our branch in Miami," she said.

"Can this be done over the phone?" I said we were in Arizona.

She suggested that we call when we were back in Florida. I said it would be a long time before we returned to Miami.

"What is your permanent address?"

"Daytona, Florida. But we don't live there."

"Where do you live?"

"On a bus."

"You're running an aviation business on a bus?"

From the tone of her voice she seemed flabbergasted. There was a pause. I asked if she was still there. She acknowledged she was, said my request was unusual, and would consult her supervisor. Then she stated somberly that the bank normally did not set up a business checking account for homeless people. I wanted to correct her, say we weren't homeless, the bus being our home, but decided against it. She called back the following day. *What was the name of our company? Why were we traveling?* I wondered if she thought we were drug dealers who laundered money. I explained our situation as best as I could. She didn't sound convinced but would get back to me.

Two days later we heard that the bank had agreed to make an exception. I didn't ask what prompted the decision. The officer wanted to know where she could fax the necessary documents for us to sign. I gave the fax number of the same *Mail Boxes Etc.* in Tucson. And once again I alerted the employees that we expected several faxes, this time from a bank in Miami. Having validated our signatures only a few days earlier, the *Mail Boxes Etc.* notary didn't know what to make of us. Legal papers, bank documents, Florida driver's licenses.

"What brought you to Tucson?"

"Just passing through," Ian said.

"Where are you staying?"

"In our bus."

"Really? You're with a film crew?"

"Yes," Ian said with a straight face, and added that we were checking out movie locations.

"What film?" the notary asked.

"Can't tell you."

Back home we joked about the way people categorized us. We'd been labeled musicians, spies, money launderers, and now film scouts.

A little Madness in the Spring is wholesome even for the King.
Emily Dickenson

With the arrival of spring, Ian and I felt light-hearted, played games with each other, hiding items on purpose, then laughing over our silly pranks. I appreciated the humor, thought there was something refreshing about an adult re-discovering the child. Over the past months, we'd let our lives get too serious, followed a hectic schedule. After returning from Canada the previous fall, we'd flown from Syracuse to Chicago to attend a retirement party, and to Miami for the inauguration of the new *Airbus Training Center.* In Northern Virginia, we'd welcomed former business associates with cocktails and canapés. Throughout October and November there'd been visits with family members and friends who appreciated the novelty of a meal served on a bus. More recently, there'd been the stressful preparation for the court case, then Ian's unexpected illness.

But leaving Arizona, we were alone and uncommitted. Ian, free of pain, his spirits lifted, rediscovered his old mischievous nature. The silliness began in Death Valley, a terrain devoid of vegetation but full of colorful primordial rocks.

With no other car in view on a straight stretch of road through the valley, Ian kept his foot on the gas pedal to see how fast our Grand Cherokee could run. I watched the speedometer. 90, 100, 105.

"You think you're on the German *Autobahn*?"

Ian grinned. "No, Death Valley. Much better." He slowed to normal speed and veered onto a narrow dirt road. I opened the sun roof, stood on the seat, and let the warm wind brush my face.

"If you want the full exposure to the sun, take your top off."

"I may just do that," and removed my T-shirt.

"You're crazy."

"Not more than you." I removed my bra.

"Look at Lady Godiva in a Jeep," Ian said, laughingly.

"So, I'm a lady now?" I sat back down.

"No you remain Miss Daisy."

"Good."

If my action was illegal, who would have seen us? Except for a few ghost towns and tiny hamlets, the region was desolate, which meant we had no access to television that evening on the bus. As always I welcomed the silence. Ian moped.

In the days that followed, we admired California's fertile valleys. Verdant fields in vivid green were in contrast to the barren desert we'd seen for the past months. Blooming fruit trees displayed glowing pink blossoms. Sheep and cows grazed on lush pastures. Ian, like a rascal enamored with noisy toys, couldn't resist disturbing the peaceful surroundings. And with childlike pleasure, my 65-year-old husband honked the bus's horns whenever we passed a meadow with cows. Mounted on top of the roof, the air horns emitted a raucous toot similar to a fog horn. Startled by the loud blast, the animals immediately raised their heads. Having their attention, Ian blew the horn again. At first I'd scolded him for disturbing the peace and accused him of turning infantile with age.

"What's wrong with greeting cows," Ian said with a sheepish grin. Passing another herd, he tooted the horn again. More irritated than frightened, the cows gazed at the bus with their mouths in perpetual motion. We ended up laughing at his ridiculous prank. One of the reasons I'd married Ian twenty-six years earlier was his ability to find humor in life.

In the mountainous terrain near Yosemite National Park, the bus's Jake brake became Ian's source of entertainment. Two-lane country roads led us over peaks and through valleys, past rural communities, and the occasional farm house on a hillside. And each time the bus approached a summit, Ian yelled *get the anchor*, then engaged the *Jake brake*, which caused the bus to pop and crackle all the way downhill, as if mini fire crackers were going off. (The brake closes the exhaust valve and causes the engine to slow.) The noise bewildered any person within close proximity. Farmers stopped their tractors and stared at our noisy rig. A mother held on to her children, as if fearing an explosion. Ian grinned, tipping his gambler hat to bystanders.

"Is all this noise necessary," I asked. I was certain the onlookers had words to say about the driver. "What if someone alerts the cops?"

"We'll be long gone." Ian assured me his maneuver wasn't illegal because the Jake brake kept the bus from accelerating downhill and running out of control.

Yosemite National Park was splendid in early spring. The freezing overnight temperatures kept visitors away. We were alone on the trails and marveled at the beauty of immense rocky peaks and powerful waterfalls. I picked yellow buttercups and bluebells for our dining table. That evening I prepared a special dinner: shephard's pie with ground lamb, topped with mashed potatoes and gratinated with cheese. As usual, I set the table with placemats and matching cloth napkins. Even in the bus, Ian and I enjoyed a sit-down meal. Civilized, we called it. And over dinner that night we reminisced about previous vacations. One of my favorites had been week-long excursions in Mackenzie riverboats down the Rogue River in Oregon and the Middle Fork of the Salmon River in Idaho. These were areas of designated wilderness undisturbed by man. Ian recalled snorkeling and deep-sea fishing in the Caribbean Sea and the Great Barrier Reef. I thought of Africa and reminded Ian of the lion that killed a giraffe in Zimbabwe and the elephant that almost attacked our car. And we talked about hunting bustards, a large running bird, in the desert of Syria. Now almost fifty years later, civil war has changed the Syria we once knew. I wonder if these birds still roam the war-stricken territory. Such adventures we had, always travelling well together.

The following morning in April 2000, we mapped our onward journey. We would avoid San Francisco and the Napa Valley, vineyards we'd visited before, and hurry into Washington State and Seattle where Ian would participate in a two-week safety audit of a major U.S airline. The work fit well in our schedule. We hoped to arrive in Canada no later than early June. By the time we reached northern California, the temperature climbed to 95 degrees; and I was eager to get farther north.

In Coburg, Oregon, the bus was to undergo some minor repairs at the Marathon Coach factory, the original place of its interior design. Ian had made an appointment to replace the sound proofing around the generator compartment and have a TV satellite antenna installed. He wanted the bus to be in perfect condition before we headed farther north. The day before the appointment, we settled at an RV park in Coburg, drove by car to the factory, and hoped for a tour. The vice-president of marketing invited us in. After the initial pleasantries, he asked about the whereabouts of our bus. Ian told him that we'd left it at an RV park.

The VP looked startled. "At an RV park?"

"Yes. What's wrong with that?" Ian asked.

"Marathon Coach owners don't park at RV parks. We have a private lot for you."

Ian said we were perfectly content where we were. But the VP insisted we drive the bus to their lot. "A vehicle like yours shouldn't be parked just anywhere."

I wanted to tell him that we'd been in worse places, but thought I'd better keep that information to myself. While he and Ian went to get our bus, I sat in the lounge and drank a cup of coffee. My thoughts went back to some of the least desirable places we'd parked. A filthy, muddy campground in Lancaster, Pennsylvania, was one. Rain had softened the ground and the bus's wheels dug deep trenches in the grass. When Ian tried to drive the bus out, mud flew everywhere. Only after a front loader threw gravel under the tires did the bus inch forward. I also remembered a parking spot in Virginia adjacent to a pig farm. The pungent odor would have appalled Marathon's VP. What about the small campgrounds in Canada and the overstuffed ones in Arizona? Printing a document on the floor at the Detroit Diesel shop in Albuquerque seemed funny months later. Obviously we didn't fit the criterion of Marathon Coach owners!

When Ian returned, we were given a tour of the factory. The VP pointed to a photo of our bus, one of a kind with its original date of delivery. He asked if we wanted business cards with the picture of our vehicle and would like to join the Marathon Travel Club. We politely declined. We didn't favor group travel, preferred to be on our own, and were heading to Canada and Alaska.

"You're taking your bus on the Alaska Highway?"

Ian asked why that was unusual. I don't remember the answer. But I do remember Ian ordered his latest toy: the most advanced retractable satellite TV antenna available. The retractable feature was important to not add height to the bus. In recent years, motion satellite television antennas have become standard equipment on most RVs. But in 2000 they were an expensive novelty. With the push of a button, Ian could raise the antenna and it automatically located the best satellite position for TV viewing. All at the cost of 8000 dollars. Only if Ian were a king, would it have made sense. Total madness, I thought.

He is happiest, be he king or peasant, who finds peace in his home.
Johann Wolfgang von Goethe

At one time or another, friends, acquaintances, and other travelers all posed the same question. "How can you give up the comfort of your house?"

Never sure how to answer, I said it had been easy. I loved to travel and loved the bus. Still, the question did puzzle me. One morning in June, I thought more deeply about it. Did I miss my house? We were in Valemount, British Columbia. Spring had arrived, its warm air welcome. I'd opened one of our lawn chairs and sat outside to enjoy the sun and a view of the snow-covered mountains. The day before I'd hiked to Kinney Lake at the foothills of Mt. Robson, the highest peak in the Canadian Rockies. Ian opted not to go. I'd met only two other hikers on an uphill trail beside a cascading stream. Near the water's edge, pink fireweed and bluebells bloomed, and giant red-stemmed cedars provided a canopy. Red squirrels moved about, and a shy marmot appeared from behind a rock. Ahead of me, majestic Mount Robson showed its white peaks. Kinney Lake is a rare place that touches the soul. Walking alone on its shores, I'd embraced the silence.

The lake's clear blue water mirrored the encircling mountains. I took several photos but knew a picture couldn't replicate the awe I felt as witness to nature's divine art.

That morning in my chair outside the bus, I looked over the sun-lit countryside and recalled Alpine meadows I'd visited as a child. I'd been too young then to appreciate their beauty. Now spectacular views enthralled me, and I thanked my good fortune for this oppor-tunity to travel. Almost a year had gone by since we'd left Florida. Had I ever missed the comfort of my house? Such a cliché. What was the appeal of comfort that so attracts people? Marketing popu-larizes the idea: Comfort Inn, comfort food, comfort colors, comfort zone. I thought about the word's meaning. In its original form, com-fort derived from Latin, *com plus fortis*, referring to giving strength and support. How does comfort relate to a house? Is a comfort zone supposed to make a person stronger or make life easier? Does the comfort of home mean less fuss, less work, less hardship? A house makes demands of its owner. It beckons to be tidied, dusted, mopped. And the surrounding yard needs planting, weeding, mowing and, depending on the region, leaf removal each fall. Not my idea of comfort. Perhaps people equate the comfort of a house to safety, a place to feel sheltered. Yet a hurricane or a tornado blows houses off their foundations. I'd witnessed the destruction in Miami. Hurricane Andrew left scattered debris where houses once stood. I recalled how power outages caused hours of discomfort during the winters we spent in Connecticut. That sunny morning, outside my bus in Valemount, I concluded that the comfort of a house is an illusion.

Could it be that belongings provide the comfort? I know that some people value themselves through possessions, clinging to them as if they were pets. I don't share their feelings. A little over a year had passed since movers packed our furnishings for storage. At the time I'd wondered if I would ever see them again. Twelve months later, the items seemed irrelevant. I'd lost interest in them. I clearly didn't miss polishing silver, washing china, and dusting knickknacks. All were unnecessary showpieces used on rare occasions. That morning, as I admired the beauty of nature, I realized that I wouldn't be upset if I never saw my prized belongings again.

Why had it taken so long to understand this? No doubt, the scenery made a difference. The view outside the bus wasn't always as pristine as that morning in British Columbia. In New Jersey, our neighbors had decorated the outside of their vehicles with multicolored lanterns and tinsel. Christmas in July they'd called it. At one RV park in California our bus was only arm's length from a neighboring vehicle. On another occasion I wondered who occupied the neighboring trailers with their plastic fences and pieces of junk under a blue tarpaulin. That day I'd stayed inside, closed the curtains, and made believe that the outside didn't exist. And the following morning I'd appreciated our ability to move on.

But now in British Columbia I recognized how much I valued the freedom of our nomadic life. Nothing tied us to a particular place. I understood why I didn't miss the *comfort of a house*. Material possessions are objects that can disappear in a flash. They provide a false sense of security, as if staking claim to something that is *mine*. Houses can fall apart. Furniture can break or blow away. Life itself is impermanent. Jobs are lost, friends and family members move away, people die. I didn't give up the *comfort of a house*. The feeling of belonging had to come from inside, not from a place or property. And for now, comfort was wherever the bus would take us.

But a few days later, I wasn't so certain.

A marriage without conflicts is
almost as inconceivable as a nation without crises.
André Maurois

I grabbed my bag and the keys to the car, said I was leaving, and stepped off the bus. Before I slammed the door behind me, I heard Ian answer, "Good." Once again our conflict had arisen from an argument over the lack of television reception. I hadn't shown sympathy for something I considered trivial. How important could the latest news be? But Ian considered a functional TV an absolute necessity.

"What if war had broken out?"

"What are you going to do about it? Re-enlist in the Air Force?"

Ian didn't like my sarcastic comment and countered it. Our words of blame escalated into fiery accusations. As our voices rose to a crescendo, the bus suddenly felt too small. I couldn't withdraw to an upstairs or downstairs, not even to a porch. The small picnic table and bench outside the vehicle wouldn't do. Why should I sit outside in the wet cold while he stayed in the warmth of our home? Under conventional circumstances, I might have visited a friend or gone shopping. But going to a shopping center in town would not divert my anger. What would I buy anyway? I needed so little. In the past I'd gone to church and played the organ, drowned out a silly feud by pulling all the stops and playing a dramatic toccata. But that afternoon in Mackenzie, a small community in central British Columbia, none of these options were available: no organ, no phone, no friend next door.

There was nothing to do but drive. I started the engine and drove from the RV park to the main highway. After a few miles, I turned onto a narrow gravel road, my destination unknown. The scenery was monotonous, the road a straight line with heavy brush and trees on both sides. I drove slowly to avoid potholes. A flat tire would be disastrous. I hoped to see a wildcat or a moose. Something to brag about later, make Ian jealous, should I ever want to be near him again. He loved wildlife safaris. We'd spent many hours watching animals in Africa and other parts of the globe. Serves him right, I thought, my eyes on the lookout for an animal. None appeared. I'd been driving for about 40 minutes when a turn-off led to a lake. I got out of the car and looked around. Not a person in sight. Not even a bird on the water. I screamed at the top of my voice, "I hate you, bastard. I can't stand you. You make me so mad."

Back in the car I continued my drive. I checked the fuel gauge. Plenty to get back home. Miles later, another lake. I stopped again, this time to stretch my back. I craved a cigarette. No doubt the rush of nicotine would calm me. I remembered its effect before I gave up smoking. The cigarette would help me think, ponder my choices. But there was no store nearby. Since leaving the RV park, I hadn't seen one. What to do? Go on driving forever? I wanted there to be an airport. I could fly away, never to return. That would serve Ian right, make him worry. But what about my home? I wasn't about to abandon it. Yet if I wanted to continue living in the bus, I needed to keep the driver. For sure I didn't want a new one.

I gazed out over the calm water, serene unlike me. Not knowing what to do next, I picked up a stick and drew lines in the mud near the water's edge. Subconsciously, each line I drew ended in a circle. Was there a message? Did it mean I couldn't break the circle of my chosen life, and that running away wasn't the answer? Still I dreaded returning to the bus. The thought of facing Ian prompted new anger. He put me in this situation. After all it had been his idea to buy the damn vehicle. Why does he need to hear the latest happenings in the world? Wouldn't once a week be enough to keep up with the news?

While I drove around the countryside, Ian, as I later learned, fumed inside the bus. He'd reached a boiling point and continued fretting over the satellite reception. Multiple times he attempted to reset the antenna. No luck. Although he'd been warned about the occasional situation when the antenna couldn't communicate with the satellite, he worried that the installation he'd paid so dearly for in Coburg was broken. And because he didn't have access to the top of the bus, he could not visually check it. Having to wait for a repair until we arrived in Anchorage was an agonizing thought. He would be at least a month without television, his only connection to the outside world. He couldn't accept it and, even worse, his wife had shown no sympathy. He rationalized that she had all *her* conveniences. He'd made sure *they* worked. But all she could do was complain about him. Bitch! He was sick and tired of always being on the losing end of the discussions and giving in to Miss Daisy's whims. That afternoon, without the television screen to keep his interest, he sat at the dining table and stared out the window. He could start the bus and move. That would serve her right. The bus would be gone when she returned. But what a drag to disconnect all the hoses and wires. Did he really want to leave? Instead he opened the refrigerator and looked for something to eat. Nothing appealed. He decided on cookies instead. He would be reproached about that, too. Putting another cookie into his mouth, he asked himself if there were anything she didn't complain about? *Why can't she leave me alone?* If she wasn't back by tomorrow morning, he would leave without her.

I didn't give him the chance. At one point I realized I had no place to go and turned around. The conflict wasn't worth giving up our home and new life. I was back four hours later.

Ian was sitting at the dining table.

"Did you have a good time?"

"Wonderful time. Saw all kinds of wildlife."

"Good. What's for dinner?"

This question had been the icebreaker in the past. Once again it ended our conflict that day. The following morning we were off to Fort Nelson and Dawson Creek, the beginning of the Alaska Highway.

A good traveler has no fixed plans and is not intent on arriving.
Lao Tzu

That summer of 2000 the bus carried us over 3000 miles, from British Columbia to Alaska and back. Low clouds hung over Dawson Creek, the starting point of the Alaska Highway. The rain had turned the ground to slush. Although eager to leave the muddy RV park behind, Ian wasn't pleased with the weather. Fog made driving hazardous, and the visibility remained limited for five hours until we reached Fort Nelson. Could be worse, I told Ian, and reminded him of the snow in Texas.

The bus's interior reeked of the onion soup I'd cooked the day before. Ian hated the obtrusive smell.

"Don't we have some deodorant spray? Bad enough I have to eat the soup."

"I'm eating it, too."

The soup was not the *soupe à l'oignon* offered in French brasseries, the one in crocks topped with a hefty slice of bread and a thick layer of melted cheese. Ours was a brew of twelve sliced onions, a stalk of minced celery, a green pepper, a few tomatoes, all boiled in a large pot of water. Desperation diet, I called it. Yet we were in agreement that something needed to be done about the extra pounds we carried. Ian in particular, as a result of taking prednisone, had gained excessive weight. Despite his complaints about the menu, we had to subsist for ten days on the soup, plus small rationings of fruit and vegetables and the occasional small portions of meat.

Two days later, north of Fort Nelson, the weather improved. I relaxed in my passenger chair and admired the scenery. Like a screen in an IMAX theater, the large windshield offered moving pictures of mountains, glaciers, rivers, and forests. For background music I selected Tchaikovsky's piano concerto No.1. No sooner had I placed the compact disc in the player, than the Tetsa River Bridge came into view. Long and narrow, it spanned a glacial river. The thought of our bus, all 20 tons of it, rolling over this narrow span of grated steel made me anxious.

"Are you sure we're going to make it across?" I felt an increase in my heart rate and hoped for a reassuring answer. Ian had a facetious smile on his face. "We'll see."

I grumbled that I didn't like him making fun of my anxiety. As the bus rolled slowly onto the open-grated passageway, the concert's pounding B-flat minor chords added befitting drama. Would there be enough room if a big vehicle came from the opposite direction?

I wanted to close my eyes, but curiosity demanded otherwise. A stream of grayish water flowed below, coniferous trees formed the shoreline. When we arrived on the other side, I took a deep breath. "Nothing to it," Ian said.

I envied my husband's casual attitude. He never panicked. Why couldn't I better control my anxiety? Since childhood, a fear of heights has made me uneasy. And on the bus in my seat, already six feet above ground, my panic worsened. While I rationalized there was nothing to fear from high places, I still trembled. If only I could turn this fright into excitement. In the weeks to come, my phobia would be tested time and again on bridges and mountainous terrain. Yet, as soon as the apparent danger was over, a triumphant thrill erased my anxiety. And now, twenty years later, I recognize the brief moments of panic added excitement to our adventure.

By then we'd been on the road for 11,000 miles, our home unscathed. I trusted Ian's ability to maneuver country roads, multi-lane highways, and mountain passes. A pre-departure briefing averted misunderstandings on routing; and Ian trusted me with the map. During long stretches he listened as I read significant, historical information in guidebooks. The Alaska and Cassiar highways are lonely roads with few towns. Originally fur trading posts for 19th century prospectors, the towns of Fort Nelson, Watson Lake, Tok, and Haines Junction are hundreds of miles apart. Even more remote are the small indigenous communities like Iskut and Dease Lake on the Cassiar Highway. Unfortunately, except for Whitehorse, Yukon's capital and largest city, the other towns disappointed us. They lacked the charm of neat little houses, small plots of vegetables and flowers, which I'd admired in the Maritime Provinces in Eastern Canada. Despite the natural splendor that Western Canada and Alaska have to offer, preservation and beauty have not been of vital interest to its inhabitants. Like their pioneers, the local population's focus is on survival, not an untainted environment.

At long last we felt no rush to be anywhere. Unlike the previous summer, Ian adapted to an easygoing schedule. We stopped arguing over directions and used our walkie-talkies for parking. And we'd given up on cellphone coverage. Except for Anchorage, Fairbanks and Whitehorse, Yukon's capital, it didn't exist. To access the Internet was just as difficult. There were times I stood in a phone booth and, with my laptop connected to the jack of the payphone, dialed the number for AOL, our internet provider, to open the website of our bank and pay bills. Email correspondence was just as tedious because of unreliable connections and interruptions. The best method to stay in touch with family and friends was a long distance phone call from a payphone, charged to a credit card.

We parked a few days on the shores of emerald Muncho Lake and fished for trout. We hiked up glacier trails and along rocky riverbeds, all the while singing and clapping to keep bears away. Years earlier while camping near Bristol Bay, Alaska, I'd learned how unpredictable these animals could be. That time a grizzly charged and, just as I'd gotten inside the float plane and closed the door, the bear pawed at the wing. This time at Muncho Lake, only one bear crossed our path, though too close for comfort. We froze in our tracks and watched the bear move on.

Ian, the aviation enthusiast, spent two hours visiting the historical Watson Lake airport, an airfield for bush pilots during the 1930s. Later it served as a refueling station for military aircraft destined for Russia during the Second World War. At the Northern Light Center I watched a film about the Aurora Borealis. For First Nations People the undulating colors in the sky represent spirits, and Wasia, the God of Light and Snow, may have been the original idea for our modern Santa Claus. And wherever I could, I picked flowers for our home. The northern hemisphere exhibits a stunning display of lupine, blue bells, Jacobs ladder, wild sweet pea, and the ubiquitous pink fireweed, as if nature devotes special energy to enhance a colorful short-growing season.

Even in the most unlikely places, we saw specks of red, blue, and yellow. And whenever I saw my late grandmother's beloved forget-me-not, I pictured her speaking to me over its pale blue petals: *Vergissmeinnicht*.

Ian and I welcomed the area's wildlife. Here and there, a shy lynx appeared, then hurried into the forest. Hungry black bears, undeterred by the bus's presence, chomped away at dandelions by the roadside.

Stone sheep made it clear that salt, leftover from clearing the highway in spring, was theirs to lick before giving us the right of way. On a turn-out near Burwash Landing, while preparing brunch, the frying bacon's scent through the kitchen's exhaust fan attracted a scrawny fox. He looked hungry and forlorn, so Ian opened the front door and offered the animal a can of French paté that we had in the refrigerator. Shy and hesitant, the animal couldn't resist the gourmet delicacy and licked the can clean.

Generally, traffic was mild the summer of 2000. I didn't need to be concerned about stop lights. Ian hadn't let me forget the day I'd yelled stop, and the doors of the refrigerator opened and emptied its shelves. Now and then road construction caused delays, the highway reduced to a single lane. Then our bus joined a long line of motorhomes, small campers, trucks, and fifth wheelers. Often unpaved, these sections of the highway smothered our bus and car with dust and mud. Although a fitted cover protected the grill and hood of the car, gravel blown from the bus's tires took out the fog lights. By the time we arrived in Alaska, both vehicles were in need of a full day's spa treatment. We soaked, scrubbed, washed, and waxed them inside and out.

One morning, over coffee, Ian studied the *Milepost*, a book that provides mile-by-mile information on every road and highway of the area. An advertisement for guided salmon charters on the Klutina River, a tributary of the Copper River, caught his attention. *Fishing Fools, and First Timers Welcome.* Ian called the number to reserve a guide one month ahead of our arrival. Copper River salmon was renowned, the best in the world. When we arrived, on July 5th, the conditions for fishing were poor. It had been raining for days, and the RV park's ground was saturated. Worse yet, unusually warm temperatures had melted glaciers that fed the river and turned it into a torrential hazard. Boating was out of the question. The guide told Ian to be patient and wait a few days for the river to calm. How long would a few days be, I wanted to know? Ian admonished me for my negative remark. He remained hopeful and went to the office every morning, expecting good news.

To pass the time I pre-cooked lasagna and steak pie, and froze them in anticipation of our children's visit. Ian and I took side trips into the Wrangell St-Elias National Park and visited Valdez. One afternoon, during a game of Scrabble on the bus, I looked out the window. Entire trees and large chunks of debris were rushing down the evermore raging river. I asked Ian how much longer we were going to stay in this swamp.

"Another day or two."

I reminded Ian about the time in New Zealand. For days we'd waited at a lodge by Lake Rotorua for the rain to stop so he could fish for trout. Conditions never improved. We returned without fish to Australia, our place of residency then.

"You had to remind me," Ian said and left to commiserate with other fishermen.

The river continued to rise. The following morning I watched in horror as the current devoured chunks of the shoreline. Ian only agreed to leave when water threatened to reach the belly of the bus. Disappointed, he headed for Anchorage. I consoled him that in Seward we would have other occasions to fish.

For the following six weeks, we shuttled between Anchorage, Seward, and Fairbanks. Three of our children visited. First to arrive were Alec and his older brother Scott, the third son from Ian's previous marriage. I'd wondered about spending two weeks on the bus with three Duncan males who shared a common gene of Scottish stubbornness. I soon discovered each had his own perception of fun, and often I was the mediator.

Alec was interested in fishing and sightseeing in style. Scott, recently divorced, liked fishing and visiting local bars. Ian hoped everyone would experience Alaska's grandeur. It started out well. In Anchorage, the hundreds of small float planes along the shore of the Lake Hood Seaplane Base intrigued Alec, our young aviator. Comparing the scene to Florida's waterways, he said Alaskans owned planes and Floridians owned boats. And on the Kenai Peninsula we visited Exit Glacier.

Though global warming wasn't a popular subject then, markers showed the glacier's annual retreat, over a mile in the past century. That day in July of 2000, we could still walk to the glacier's terminus and follow a trail over the mighty blue ice. Unfortunately, as I recently read, that is no longer possible due to the warming atmosphere and the retreating glacier.

In Seward, Scott enticed Alec to go bar hopping. Hungover and tired the following morning, they hoped early fog and rain would cause the cancelation of our fishing charter. Ian had paid for a private boat, and their lack of interest upset him. To prevent a nasty conflict, I insisted they go. The weather improved. Their mood changed as soon as the fish began to bite. By noon we'd caught our limit of six silver salmon each.

Five days later, at Denali National Park, we debated if the daylong bus ride into the Preserve was worth the trip. Alec didn't think so. Was I kidding, he wanted to know, eleven hours, on a school bus? Reluctantly, he took a seat next to his brother and busied himself with the video camera. According to my diary, we saw eighteen bears, several caribou, foxes, sheep, a moose, and varied scenery. Regardless of Alec's aversion to the school bus, the hours passed quickly.

The following day we moved on to Fairbanks. From 25 years earlier, I recalled the little frontier town with its small shops, bars, and a diner along the main street near the banks of the Chena River. Fairbanks had been a stop-over point on Pan American's flight from New York to Tokyo. In the years since, the town had grown into sprawling city of highways and strip malls. The Museum of the University of Alaska, a modern architectural marvel, was not the small building I recalled from the winter of 1972. Yet the rivers and lakes hadn't changed. Alec and Scott enjoyed excellent trout fishing and, before flying home, they befriended a pair of red foxes on Fort Wainwright Army Base.

Three weeks later in mid-August, Natasha arrived in Anchorage with her girlfriend Veronika. No suitcases this time, only backpacks. They'd barely settled in the bus when Natasha's agent called from New York City. My daughter had recently become a model for the Wilhelmina agency. The client hoped to cast Natasha for a bra ad and needed a current photo in underwear right away. In 2000 I didn't have a cell phone to take a quick image and send it at a moment's notice. Nor were digital cameras popular. Film needed developing, photos printed. Since the bus was parked on Elmendorf Air Force Base, Ian drove us to a remote location, a small lake in the woods. I took several photos, which were printed. Natasha mailed them overnight to her agent and was given the job.

For the next ten days the bus took us once again from Seward to Fairbanks. Instead of fishing, we chartered a boat to watch wildlife and see glaciers calve. Puffins flew by, whales surfaced, otters and porpoises swam alongside the boat. Sea lions grunted and growled at us from an offshore island. Northeast of Anchorage, Natasha, Veronika, and I hiked on the Matanuska glacier. Wearing crampons, we'd crossed turquoise clear rivulets, walked by glacial pools and crevasses, and watched water disappear into deep moulins.

And a few days later, the girls didn't mind riding the school bus in Denali National Park. Ian commented how the park had changed in the past three weeks. Grasses had turned ocher and red. Bears no longer looked for grubs on the green hillsides but fed on soapberries along the riverbeds. A lone wolf on the road howled as if searching for his pack. It had snowed overnight on the higher elevations and the Eielson Visitor Center was a winter wonderland. About midday the sky cleared and exposed a rare unobstructed view of snow-covered Mt. McKinley.

Back in Fairbanks, the girls panned for gold at Dredge No 8. A vial with Natasha's gold flakes sits on my desk today. At the Malemute Saloon, a rustic bar with sawdust on the floor, we watched hilarious comic acts about the gold rush days. On our last night together, we ate dinner at the Pump House and shared left-overs with the same red foxes that Alec and Scott had befriended.

With the summer nearly over, Ian and I were by ourselves again. Natasha called from New York to say she'd arrived safely and was flying to Lisbon for a modeling shoot. She missed the stillness of Alaska and lamented that she found the noise and traffic in Manhattan irritating. Alec also was in touch. After returning to Daytona, he completed his first cross-country flight to Oklahoma City and back. Scott loved Alaska so much that five years later he ended up being stationed at Elmendorf Air Force Base.

At the end of August, the Fairbanks campground which three weeks earlier had bustled with people, emptied. The bus stood alone. The owner of the RV park was ready to close for winter and warned us about snow. Not again, I thought. Ian was sure the man exaggerated. The past few days had been sunny with temperatures in the mid-sixties. I mentioned that I'd heard Ian's prognosis before and said it was time to leave. We'd driven every navigable road in Alaska. On August 31st we left on our 2,300-mile journey southbound for Prince Rupert on the coast of British Columbia.

Ian's weather prediction was correct. Except for some light flurries near Whitehorse, we didn't encounter snow on our way south. In the Yukon, fall colors greeted us. The French writer, Albert Camus, had written that autumn is a second spring when every leaf is a flower. The fireweed we saw had lost its bright pink blossoms. Its leaves and stems had turned crimson and formed a colorful border alongside the highway. Black spruces stood like lonely statues amid red and burnt-orange grasses. Here and there, yellow leaves still hung on white birch trees. Ian, in a hurry to get south, allowed the bus little rest. A one-lane Timber Bridge awaited us on the Cassiar Highway.

"Turbulence ahead, fasten your seatbelt," Ian said, as we approached the narrow span.

The passage resembled a relic from Western movies, just wide enough for one carriage.

I grabbed the armrests. "Please go slowly."

"Why? So you have plenty of time to look down?"

Again I didn't appreciate my husband's humor. Pots, pans, and dishes rattled as the bus bounced across a pothole and hit the wooden

decking. Wet from an earlier shower, the bridge looked slippery. But as he'd done before, Ian kept his composure and eased the bus over the bridge's wooden slats, 130 feet above the river. Once across, I breathed relief.

Ian wanted to drive to Hyder, a hamlet located NW of Ketchikan at the end of a seventy-mile fjord bordering Alaska and British Columbia. Someone had told him about bears and salmon in Hyder. As if we hadn't seen enough of them that summer! Only one road leads to Hyder, a four-hour roundtrip from Meziadin Junction in British Columbia on the Glacier Highway. The scenery, though magnificent, was déjà vu. We'd seen enough glaciers, listened to their sounds, watched them calve. Ian was more interested in dinner. "I feel like having pumpkin pie for dessert. Don't we have one in the freezer?"

"Yes, but it takes over an hour to bake. It'll be too late by the time we reach the RV park."

"You could bake it *en route.*"

I turned on the oven, placed the pie inside, and again took my seat up front. Forty-five minutes later, the odor of burnt pumpkin made me hurry to the kitchen. On the rack was an empty brown pie shell, its contents on the oven's walls.

"Oh shit." I grumbled, turned off the oven, and closed the door.

"What's the matter?"

"No pumpkin pie tonight."

"Why."

"Did it ever occur to you that the frozen custard, once thawed, would become runny and spill during the rough ride? That's what happened. A giant mess."

Ian didn't react. I put on potholders, threw the burnt pie shell in the trash and hoped we reached Hyder soon. Ian was lamenting his failed pie. Once the oven had cooled, I spent the remainder of the drive scraping burnt pumpkin from the oven's walls.

A green sign on a post alerted us that we were entering Alaska. No border control, no immigration, no Custom's office. The gravel road led past a U.S. post office, a general store, a bar, and eventually to a small campground. As so often in the past, the bus prompted the curiosity of the locals: *Who are you? What brings you here?* Fewer than one hundred people lived in this tiny outpost. Once again, Ian gave the story that we were scouting for movie locations. A film about bears and fish in Alaska. One fellow was quick to point out that we'd come to the right place. There was an area outside of town, he told us, where we could see more bears and salmon than anywhere in the world. Fish creek, they called it. As we discovered the following day, the setting was surreal. Hundreds of salmon were spawning in the creek's shallow waters, their final resting place. The putrid smell of dead fish was so unbearable I held a scarf over my nose. Several black bears, undeterred by the foul odor and oblivious to our presence, stood in the shallow water and scooped up fish to fill their stomachs. I wasn't sure I ever wanted to eat salmon again.

The day we prepared to leave, a fellow asked Ian when we would return. Had we seen the bears and the fish? Had we been to the local bar and enjoyed some of their powerful brew? Did we know that in Hyder there was no law enforcement because there was no crime? Ian assured the man that we would be back soon. We had no desire to return, continued south to Prince Rupert. I'd booked a passage on a ferry boat to Vancouver Island for the 9th of September.

Now I must take my reader back in time, to the onset of that summer in 2000, to share a few episodes of our Canadian and Alaskan adventures.

Geography of British Columbia

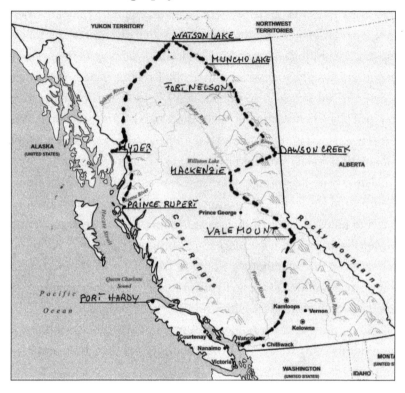

I admire anyone that follows the road less traveled.
Kevin McCloud

Once again Ian longed to travel by car to the far north. Taking the bus from Dawson City to Canada's Northwest Territories and the Arctic Ocean was out of the question. A ruptured tire could leave us stranded for days. But we were told the 500-mile unpaved Dempster Highway, as the road is called, was also risky by car, that we should carry at least two spare tires, that it could be a day or two before another vehicle passed by. We would be stuck in desolate territory and the target of vicious, giant mosquitos. Yet the naysayers couldn't deter Ian. He imagined the trip as not anymore arduous as previous ones. Could the road be worse than the one we'd driven to Goose Bay the previous summer? And this wasn't our first time venturing into uninhabited northern territory. Twenty years earlier, we'd camped in the wild near Bristol Bay in SW Alaska, a site only accessible by float plane. This time we would stay in motels listed in our guidebook: the Mackenzie Hotel in Inuvik, a town 120 miles north of the Arctic Circle, and the Sunshine Inn, located in a tiny settlement on the confluence of the Mackenzie and Arctic Red River. We would leave the bus in Tok, Alaska, drive back to Canada via the Taylor Highway, and take a ferry over the Yukon River to Dawson City. Ian didn't foresee any obstacles.

Long before our departure, Ian urged me to make hotel reservations. I questioned the need. Who that summer of 2000 would be in-
clined to travel to these outposts? But Ian insisted. His airline career
had spoiled him. Wherever he landed, a hotel room was assured.
Now in retirement he still liked the guarantee of a bed and meal after
a long drive. We were still in British Columbia early in June, when I
placed a call from a payphone to the Sunshine Inn in Tsiigehtchic.
To my surprise, the call went through. A woman answered. I said I
wanted to reserve a room for one night on June 28th.

"The owner not here."

"When will he be back?"

"Dunno. He out hunting."

"Shall I call back tomorrow?"

"A week. Maybe a week he be back."

I hung up and told Ian about my conversation. He wondered what
kind of animal the man was hunting in spring. A week later I called
again. The same woman answered.

"The owner out hunting."

This can't be, I thought. "Can *you* take a reservation?"

"Yes."

"I need a room for June 28. One night".

"OK."

"Did you understand? One night. June 28."

"OK."

"Don't you need my name?"

"What?"

"My name to reserve a room. Duncan is the name."

"Yes."

I wondered if she understood any of it. "Do you need a credit card
number to hold the reservation?"

"Credit?"

"My Mastercard."

"OK."

"Can you copy down the number?"

"Number. Yes."

I gave her my credit card number, speaking slowly several times. Each time she answered with *yes*.

"See you on June 28."

"OK." That ended the call. Luckily the Mackenzie Hotel clerk in Inuvik was not out hunting and took my reservation on the first try.

Two weeks later, early on June 28th, we set out from Dawson City to Tsiigehtchic. In the car were gallons of drinking water, mosquito repellant, cans of tuna, sardines, crackers, cheese, and cookies. The Thule rooftop carrier held a tent, rain gear, blankets, sleeping bags, and toilet paper. Our first stop would be a service station in Eagle Plains, 250 miles north, then another 150 miles to Tsiigehtchic. Ian estimated a mid-afternoon arrival. The guide book calculated the trip to be over twelve hours but didn't give a reason. Ian didn't believe it and said the guidebook's writer must have traveled in a backfiring Tin Lizzie. He counted on dinner that night in Tsiigehtchic, early to bed, and an easy drive of two to three hours to Inuvik the following day. I told him to curtail his optimism. We weren't far outside of Dawson City when coarse dirt forced Ian to slow down.

"I see why people told us to take two spare tires," I said.

"We only have one. Can't drive faster than thirty miles per hour to be safe."

"Maybe the writer hadn't driven a Tin Lizzie after all."

"You always think you know everything."

I didn't respond. An argument would make this day even longer. A den of foxes by the road brightened our mood. Ian stopped. Young kits were chasing each other, coming in and out of their burrow. We counted five or six. Farther up the road, a lynx crossed in front of us. Furtive by nature, it soon disappeared in the woods. Our drive the previous year through Labrador came to mind, without the roller-coaster peaks. I'd thought then we had traveled the most lonesome road of North America. Maybe we hadn't. Somewhere I'd read that Canada's problem was excessive land, which had become a burden. I wondered how natural land could be an encumbrance. The wilderness along the Dempster Highway seemed endless, particularly from mountain ridges. In spite of the season, some of the rivers were still partially frozen. The high content of iron oxide in the Ogilvie River had colored the ice reddish pink, as if a river of blood.

A sign announced an emergency airstrip. A runway? Here?

"Anyone on final approach?" Ian asked, jokingly.

I looked out the window. "Not that I see."

A windsock appeared, the road widened, and orange barrels, labeled fifty gallons AVGAS, appeared.

"What are they for?"

"Emergency fuel for the rookie bush pilot who got lost and ran low on fuel," Ian said. He figured the runway at 3000 feet. Before the day's end, we would encounter several more airstrips.

North of the Arctic Circle, the black pine forests gave way to miles of green hillsides. From a distance they looked to be dusted with snow. A closer look revealed arctic cotton in full bloom.

We stopped for a picnic by the roadside, thankful for the light breeze to keep mosquitos away. A Ptarmigan inched toward us. Its plumage of mottled brown and black feathers blended well with the surrounding grasses. Curious to make our acquaintance, the bird chattered away. I tried mimicry to encourage a longer conversation while Ian videoed our unique repartee.

"I must be crazy talking to a bird."

"I always knew you were strange. Now you're cuckoo."

"I guess that's what happens when surrounded by wilderness."
"Gives you a taste of what explorers felt," Ian said, adding that the bird might not have encountered a human before.

We were miles from civilization. There was silence. No town. No noise of an approaching car, not a sound except the light whisper of the wind. The bird wandered off, leaving us alone in the wild. Overcome with awed respect for nature, we savored the solitude a while longer, then resumed our journey. Back in the car, Ian remembered the fellow in Labrador, the one who traveled with his rooster. "Maybe he wasn't so crazy after all."

By mid-afternoon we reached the Peel River, the first of two major river crossings. Ahead of us, a bulldozer was pushing heaps of mud, in order to form a passable landing for the ferry. I was aghast. A mudslide to get on the boat? First in line, a pick-up truck, slid down sideways. The bulldozer pushed more mud in place, and it was our turn. Though in 4-wheel drive, our Cherokee began to swerve in all directions. Ian had to spin the steering wheel three revolutions left then back to right several times, to keep it from fishtailing through the mud.

"Must have felt like landing an airplane in strong crosswind," I said once we were safely on the ferry.

"Worse."

Ninety minutes later we approached the Mackenzie River, a wider expanse of water than I'd imagined. Way off to my right on a bluff, Tsiigehtchic became visible. The village appeared tiny, forlorn in the wilderness. I wondered about the Sunshine Inn? Had the owner returned from hunting? Was there a restaurant nearby? Ian was tired and hungry. I welcomed the easy access to the ferry. No mudslide. Once on board, Ian and I got out of the car to stretch and enjoy the cool breeze.

"Going straight across," the ferry operator announced.

"No," I yelled. "We are going to Tsiigehtchic." From the guidebook, I knew the ferry was supposed to make a stop there before crossing to the far side of the Mackenzie River.

He gave me an incredulous frown. "You sure?"

"Yes, we have a reservation at the Sunshine Inn."

"Nobody goes there." He walked around our vehicle and used his heavy glove to clear the dirt from our license plate. "Florida, hey?"

"Yes," Ian said.

"Why would you come from Florida to Tsiigehtchic? You on the run from the police?"

"No, just regular tourists."

"Yeah, right." He shook his head, gave us a look as if we were crazy or drug dealers, or both. "Good luck," he said as we approached the spit of land.

A dirt road led up a hill into the village, past some shacks and tepees. Ian asked me about directions to the motel. I told him all I had was a street and a number. But the streets were not marked, no motel in sight.

Ian was getting annoyed. "Roll down your window and ask."

"Who?"

"Don't act so stupid."

I waved at a man in front of a shanty. "Where is the Sunshine Inn?"

All he did was shake his head. It hadn't occurred to me yet that the people in the community spoke nothing but Gwich'in, their native tongue. I told Ian that I was not getting out of the car. If he wanted to inquire about the inn, he would have to do it. Ian parked, disappeared in a native community hall. A few minutes later he was back, visibly distraught. "There is no Sunshine Inn."

"It can't be."

"Doesn't exist." Ian put the car in gear, floored the pedal. With honking horn and flashing headlights we raced back to the landing.

The ferry was waiting. With a triumphant smile, the operator said he thought we'd be back. Ian didn't respond, then looked at me. "You'd told me that you spoke with someone and made a reservation."

"I did. The woman accepted my credit card."

"You better hope there are no charges."

I was still dumbfounded. "Who told you there is no Sunshine Inn?"

Ian said an older man with some knowledge of English told him the inn long ceased to exist, then offered his home to spend the night. I said that was nice of him. Ian looked at me sideways. "Staying in some shack? I didn't think so."

Three minutes later we were off the ferry and back on the road. I suggested pulling out the tent and sleeping bags.

"No. We're continuing to Inuvik."

"That's two, three more hours."

"I'm not sleeping by the roadside."

"At least we have daylight," I said, recalling how we'd driven the year before to Labrador City in the dark.

At ten that night, when we walked into the lobby of the Mackenzie Hotel in Inuvik, I felt nervous. *Please let there be a room.* Not only was the hotel fully booked, there was no record of our reservation for the following day. Impossible, I thought. This wasn't a small hotel. I figured it held about 100 rooms on two levels. *Why so many guests? Was there a pow-wow?* Ian went into orbit. I'd hoped he would let me deal with the clerk. I don't remember what was said or what I did, but a room suddenly became available. Then we heard an apology. The restaurant had closed. But down the road was an all-night diner. At eleven p.m. a dubious crowd was there. We ate a burger, French fries with Poutine, and hurried back to the hotel.

The following morning we discovered Inuvik, the People's Place. Numerous bridges crossed over large, above ground conduits that carried sewer and water to most buildings. Perfect for sled riding in winter, I thought. We drove by the airport and walked along the harbor and river. Inuvik's main attraction was the *Igloo* church. Missionaries without formal plans had built the church from wood floated 1200 miles down the Mackenzie River. Even though the structure was built without pilings, permafrost never caused the church to shift, not since its opening in 1960. An architectural miracle, we were told.

Later that day in the lobby, Ian overheard a couple inquiring about chartering a plane to a village on the Arctic Ocean and back. Would anyone be interested in sharing the cost? Ian was, in an instant. We set a departure for early the following morning and ate dinner at the hotel. I regretted ordering a muskox burger. The meat was tough, and the sauce couldn't disguise the gamey flavor. But Ian enjoyed a steak.

The following morning, in the Piper Aztec, Ian sat next to the pilot on the 30-minute flight to Tuktoyaktuk, a village 90 miles north of Inuvik. The other couple occupied the two window seats to my left, I sat behind Ian. Looking down over the wide Mackenzie River delta, I noticed some dome-shaped hills and asked the pilot if they were volcanoes.

He said they were pingos, soil-covered ice domes, caused by frost heaves. He went on to say the entire area freezes over in the fall, and local daredevils compete to be the first to drive on the ice from Inuvik to Tuktoyaktuk. I didn't ask how many failed to make it.

Simon, a local guide, welcomed the four of us to Tuktoyaktuk, which I learned later translates into *resembling a caribou*. The Arctic Sea was still partially frozen that day, June 30th, and the few hundred residents were eagerly awaiting a thaw and the return of whales whose meat they depended on. Simon showed us the "icehouse," an underground community freezer cut into the permafrost, then led us a few yards to a levee with cottages. Summer residences, he explained. Soon the townspeople would move there and attend to their smokehouses. A short summer, I thought.

While we walked around the village, I commended Simon for his good English. Most people in the northern regions speak in their native tongues. Simon said he hadn't spoken English until he started school. I told him that English wasn't my first language either, and that I spoke several.

Simon looked surprised. "You mean people can speak more than one language?"

"Yes. So can you."

He said I was the first person he'd met who spoke more than two languages and wondered which one he should learn next.

"French. It's beautiful."

Simon looked excited. He would try to learn it.

Although the local population hadn't converted to Christianity, Tuktoyatuk has a Catholic and an Anglican church. People incorporated Christian beliefs with their Gods of nature. The Anglican, a log cabin with a woodstove in its center was the oldest. Sealskin covered both the altar and a small organ. I opened a Bible and saw the text in Iqualit. I asked Simon if all of the townspeople went to church.

"Of course," he said, "It's for entertainment. Standing room only."

Before we left Tuktoyaktuk I received a certificate for dipping my foot into the cold Artic waters. Ian declined. Simon's last words to me: He was going to learn a third language!

Now twenty years later, I wonder what attracted us to the northern regions. What made us drive the distant lonely road to Inuvik, 120 miles north of the Arctic Circle? Travel websites such as TripAdvisor were in their infancy then. Tourists did not leave personal reviews on-line. A Canadian guidebook devoted only one page to the area, but the map showed a road. And we had wanted to discover where it would take us.

On our way back to Dawson City, we stopped several times on a high ridge, always in awe of the vast uninhabited land. We hiked across a meadow abloom with white Arctic cotton, and admired the occasional parrya, a small purplish flower, which grows between cracks of rocks and defies the odds of survival.

We were not eager to re-enter the world of traffic and noise. In love with unspoiled nature, stillness, a sighing wind, the two of us alone, we agreed the north had a magical appeal: the mysterious darkness and harsh weather in winter, the astonishing beauty during the summer months, recounted Robert Service's poem *Spell of the Yukon:*

> *It's the great, big, broad land 'way up yonder,*
>   *It's the forests where silence has lease;*
>   *It's the beauty that thrills me with wonder,*
>   *It's the stillness that fills me with peace*

Geography of the Yukon Territory

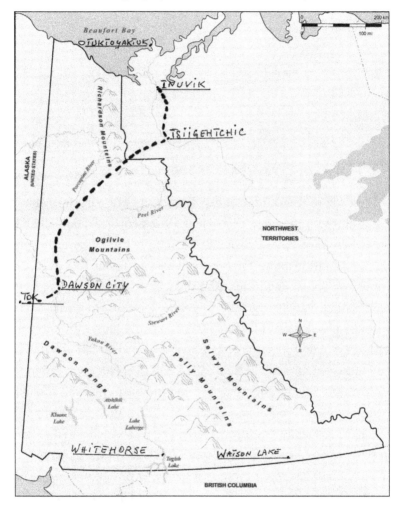

Gossip is conversation about people.
Gore Vidal

I quickly realized the laundry room in an RV park was akin to a waiting room at a doctor's office. Most people would rather be somewhere else. Some customers entertained their own thoughts and sat quietly waiting for the machines to finish. Others leafed through outdated magazines. And there were those who longed for conversation, usually small talk or gossip. I listened to stories of children, grandchildren, and pets. Men rarely did laundry, although a few helped their wives carry baskets. But no sooner had the baskets been unloaded, than these men exited as if the place were forbidden territory. Ian was no different. Did the male ego prohibit this type of work? Or was it because women didn't trust their husbands with the task? Personally, I never minded doing wash, a chore I'd enjoyed since childhood. And I liked to iron. The sight of me ironing in an RV park's laundry room prompted sarcastic remarks. *Look, she is ironing. Can you believe it?* One woman asked if my husband forced me to do this. I answered with a smile and said I enjoyed the task. I could tell the woman thought I was nuts.

The afternoon when I entered the laundry room in Tok, Alaska, we'd returned from Dawson City and the Northwest Territories. The facility was unusually busy, several machines in use. A woman in a pink T-shirt sat idly in a chair. Another, wearing a baseball cap, was bent over a magazine. Three more stood talking to each other near a folding table. I said hello. They looked at me for a moment, returned the greeting, and continued their conversation. I sensed they had known each other before or traveled in a convoy.

Tired from the six-hour journey that day from Dawson City, I was not in the mood for idle chat. First, there'd been the queue to get onto the ferry to cross the Yukon River, then a treacherous drive over the dirt-ridden Taylor Highway. This "Top of the World Highway" winds along a mountain range to the U.S. border. Although the views were breathtaking, the steep inclines and lack of guard rails caused my usual anxiety. Ian, in a hurry to get home, had been driving faster than I considered safe. Back in Tok at the RV park, we unloaded the car before Ian set out to wash it. A real mess, its color unrecognizable after the drive to Inuvik, with mud caked beneath the wheel wells, and grime covering the interior. The seals on doors and windows had been inadequate to keep out dust, which also passed through the air circulation filters. I figured it would take an entire day and multiple wet rags to wipe every nook and cranny. But better to wait and start early the following day. So I'd resorted to doing the laundry, a less cumbersome chore. And while waiting for the wash, I thought to update my diary. But no sooner had I put my laundry in the machine and sat down, than the pink T-shirted woman wanted to talk and asked where I was from.

"Florida."

"How long did it take you to get to Alaska?"

"We've been on the road for over a year?"

"You haven't been home since?" She said it so loud that everyone looked at me.

"The RV is my home."

One of the women at the folding table said, "What about Christmas?" You weren't home for Christmas?"

"No."

The questions continued. How had I done my Christmas shopping? Didn't I have family? Children? Grandchildren? I said I had both. Her companion lamented there wasn't enough space in her RV to store presents. She usually started her Christmas shopping in July, but now had to wait until September when she would be home. She also collected Beanie Babies, a fad in the late nineties. Some travelers placed them across the dashboard of their RVs. I wanted to say that shopping was not my purpose in life but held the thought back and asked my laundry room companions about their travels. Everyone agreed the scenery was superb. The woman wearing a baseball cap had liked Dawson City. I said that I, too, had been enchanted with the historic town on the Yukon and Klondike Rivers, where gold mining men set foot 100 years earlier. I described how I'd walked every street and admired the buildings, old and new, constructed in the style of the town's glory days during the gold rush. Had she seen the Gaslight Follies, a vaudeville play about that era? She said it was entertaining and funny. But we agreed that Tom Byrne's Robert Service Show was the best in town. I asked if she'd bought a mammoth tusk carving. She hadn't but mentioned the delicious ice cream. I recalled how Ian and I, ice cream cones in hand, had strolled at 10 p.m. along the bank of the Yukon River.

Now, 20 years later, curious about changes in Dawson City, I have searched the Internet. Thomas Byrne celebrated his 90th birthday in 2014 and has stopped performing. Park rangers at Robert Service's cabin recite his poetry, though I doubt with the same effect. And the curtain closed long ago on the gaslight follies. But I was happy to read that the recently refurbished Palace Theater has reopened.

That afternoon at the laundry in Tok, time passed quickly. Before placing the wash in a dryer I'd noted down some of the past days' highlights. Had any of the women ever listened to the silence? Or talked with a bird? Felt the wonder of nature's vast domain? I didn't think the washroom was the place to ask. I placed my laundry in a dryer and watched the items tumble. A new couple entered, husband and wife I assumed. He set the heavy basket down, then left. His wife was ready to talk as soon as she'd figured out how to operate the machine. Where was everyone going? Where had we been? How did we stay warm? She lamented the freezing temperatures in the Yukon. The T-shirted woman said the cold wasn't as bad as the hours of daylight. How can anyone sleep, when it's sunny at eleven p.m.?

"Eye shades," I said, and asked where she'd been.

"Drove here from Dawson City. A scary road. And lots of dust."

"Yes," I said, and mentioned that our vehicle was covered with grime and dirt.

"But that's not the worst," she said. "You should have seen the crazy drivers."

"Really?"

"There was that guy in a Jeep Grand Cherokee going sixty miles per hour downhill."

Oh no, I thought. No doubt, they were talking about Ian. I'd been upset when he shifted gears and passed a long line of campers and small motorhomes.

The women near the folding table chimed in. "I bet it was the same guy who passed us."

"Were you coming down the Taylor Highway?"

"Yes."

The baseball cap woman had seen it, too. "He passed us at great speed, trailing a cloud of dust."

"Yes, that must have been him."

"And he kept on going. Almost pushed us off the road."

I had the awful feeling that if I stayed long enough in the laundry room someone would connect me with that crazy person in the Jeep Grand Cherokee. Without saying a word, I quickly took my clothes, dry or not, out of the dryer, wished the ladies a good evening and a safe journey. Back home I told Ian that he better hope no one recognized our car because a bunch of women at the laundry room were outraged about his driving. I said I'd heard them talking about *some guy* in a Jeep Grand Cherokee nearly running their campers off the road on the Taylor Highway. Ian thought the accusations were funny. I didn't see the humor. Then he reassured me that no one would recognize the car, washed and restored to its original color.

I didn't see the women again. But laundry rooms continued to be entertaining places where I would meet a blend of people, mostly happy travelers seeking adventure. But few were on the road full time.

Nikaitchuatǵuuq piraqtut.
(Those who think they can, will accomplish something)
Iñupiat saying

We were in Fairbanks early in August, our sons had left, and Natasha wasn't due to arrive for another ten days. What to do next? I suggested we take the car to the North Slope. Ian was not interested and reminded me about our long drive to Inuvik five weeks earlier. Did I really want to tackle another ride on gravel? Except for the North Slope, we'd been on every road in Alaska, most recently to Circle Hot Springs, which Ian regarded as a disappointing six-hour round trip. The highlight was a moose and her baby by the roadside.

But the historic resort hotel and its surroundings appeared so neglected that we didn't bathe in the hot mineral waters. Still, I thought taking the road to Prudhoe Bay would be our last chance to see more of Alaska's wilderness. Ian remained unenthusiastic. He wasn't going to drive 500 miles each way to see oilfields and a bunch of tract houses. The car would be covered with dust and grime and we'd spend two days cleaning it. I told Ian there would be the Gates of the Arctic National Park, an unpopulated, mountainous terrain the size of Switzerland. On flights from Fairbanks to Tokyo I'd admired the rugged peaks. To entice Ian, I showed him pictures in a guidebook, suggested a float trip on one of the park's rivers. He remained undeterred about driving there. But if I insisted on seeing that part of Alaska, we could charter a small plane and fly to the region.

He contacted Curly, a former Pan American pilot, who each spring flew his Cessna 180 from Fort Lauderdale to Fairbanks. I'd met him years earlier. Why the name Curly? Ian said the name was a joke among his pilot friends because Curly's hair was cut so close to the scalp. He agreed to a full-day charter, a roundtrip of 600 miles.

Early in the morning a few days later, the three of us took off from Metro Field Airport, a few miles outside of Fairbanks. I wasn't aware of a flight plan and didn't ask how long we would be in the air, or where Curly planned to land. For me the experience wasn't unusual. Years before I'd gone flying with Ian and a pilot friend in a float plane over southern Alaska, soaring through narrow passes, then landing on remote lakes to fish for trout. Once we'd landed on a glacier to collect ice for our drinks. The thrill of going along preempted questions. This time was not different, in the back seat behind two knowledgeable pilots. I liked Curly, a charming fellow with an infectious smile and a terrific sense of humor. A little over an hour later we landed in Bettles, a small airstrip at the foothills of the Brooks Range. I asked what we were doing.

"Pit stop," Ian said, which meant he needed a bathroom.

Curly led us a short distance to a large log cabin and said we would get a great breakfast there. Backpacks and camping gear lined the entrance. People who had returned from canoeing crowded the restaurant. Unfortunately, every table was taken. We had to forgo breakfast but ordered sticky cinnamon rolls and three cups of coffee to go. With nothing else to do, we were soon airborne.

Ian commented on the perfect weather conditions: no wind, blue sky. Our little Cessna flew between peaks of the Brooks Range, and I, camera in hand, admired the velvety green summits.

Here and there, snow remained in crevasses. A few Dall sheep grazed in the meager grasses. The splendid scenery held my full attention, and I forgot my cinnamon roll, still in its wrap. Thirty minutes later, I overheard Curly say there should be an airport around the next mountain. I bent forward and looked over Ian's shoulder, ready to spot a runway. But no airport came into view.

"Must have been the wrong mountain," Curly said, and turned the plane around. Ian studied the chart on his lap. A creek below meandered through a valley. Up front Curly and Ian joked around. I

didn't dare inquire what was funny. But I wondered about the airport. Was there a need for one here? In the wilderness?

"Where are we going?" I finally asked.

"Don't worry," Ian said. "A little airfield in the mountains."

"Why are we landing there?"

"To stretch our legs," he said, teasing me.

I should have known better than to ask. Long ago I'd learned that pilots fly for the sake of being in the air. The destination is secondary. I kept on the lookout for an airfield. *Had we flown over this area before?* I couldn't tell. For the next fifteen minutes, the countryside changed little, the mountains looked familiar. *Could we be lost?* I had a brief uneasy feeling that we might not find a way out of the mountainous maze, but pushed the thought away. After all, these two experienced pilots had found their way in the dark to airports around the world. They should be able to locate a small airfield under a clear sky.

Had we not eventually landed in Anaktuvuk Pass, a small Nuna-miut community, our excursion to the North Slope would have been just another airplane ride. Curly parked the Cessna and suggested we take a walk. A dirt road led past small sod-huts. The peaceful hamlet looked lost in time. Not one store, not a person around. Curly said most men were probably out hunting. Ian needed a bathroom. I asked where he imagined finding one? At a gas station? A café? We walked aimlessly a few hundred feet or more. A side road led to a modern log structure.

Was it a residence? It looked different from the other dwellings. Ian was sure he would find a bathroom inside. We entered what was a museum.

"Paġlan," a young woman in her early twenties said, welcoming us. I was taken by her lovely face and beautiful smile. While the men wandered through the museum, I engaged Vera in conversation. She was eager to talk about her people and told me about the Iñupiat (the word translates into *real people*), their language, and Simon Paneak, who founded the community.

"Why the name Anaktuvuk Pass?"

"Place of many Caribou droppings." Vera said, explaining the caribou were her people's main food supply. The herds passed through the area in fall and returned in spring to their calving grounds on the North Slope. Vera said during hunting season, the entire village butchered the animals.

"We have a big feast," she said. "No waste!"

Before settling in Anaktuvuk Pass, Vera's people had been nomads. Instead of a house, they viewed the land as their home. I said my husband and I were also nomads, permanent travelers without a homestead. Vera seemed curious, yet without envy. She had never left her village but would love to see more of the world. Eager to learn, she had taken courses over the Internet and hoped to earn a master's degree. Our backgrounds couldn't have been more different; and yet we connected. I took a liking to this young woman and her inquisitive mind, and praised her ambition. I sensed she felt the same about me. Over the years I've wondered about the mysterious force that creates such a bond. I felt as if I'd known this young woman before and were speaking to an old friend. Was this what Carl Jung meant by the collective unconscious?

When I told Vera that Anaktuvuk Pass reminded me of Tuktoyaktuk, the tiny coastal community Ian and I had visited in Canada's Northwest Territories, I felt her excitement.

"You've been to Tuktoyaktuk?"

"Yes, a month ago."

"I would love to go one day." She had family there, but only her mother had been to Tuktoyaktuk. She wanted to know more. How did we get there? What did we do?

That day I didn't know the exact distance between Tuktoyaktuk and Anaktuvuk Pass. About 500 air miles, I learned later. By sled in winter the trip could take several weeks. By air, with no direct service, it would have taken two days or more. I told Vera how we'd driven to Inuvik and taken a 30-minute flight over the Mackenzie River delta to Tuktoyaktuk. She wanted to know if I'd spoken with anyone in the village. I told her about Simon, the young guide who had shown us around. I said he was of slim build with a pleasant face, that his five siblings lived in the village. A proud member of his community, he had spoken excellent English, which he didn't learn until he started school. Vera was sure her mother knew of him.

Ian put a sudden end to our conversation. "Are you ready to go?"

I said I would be shortly after I saw the museum's attractive display of local artifacts. Before we left, I told Vera that I would be in touch one day, and she invited me back.

As the plane lifted off I looked down over the village, took one last photo, then envisioned the place in winter, devoid of color, an image in black and white. How this tiny community can endure the isolation, the hours of darkness, and the white expanse under snow still puzzles me. We headed farther north, away from the mountains, a flat grassy tundra below. I felt hungry and devoured the sticky bun. Our next stop was Umiat, an airstrip for hunters to use during caribou season.

The sole resident of this outpost lived with his dog in a shack by the runway. He introduced himself as John and, eager to make conversation, offered us iced tea. Surprised how hot it was that day, I welcomed the cool drink. John said the heat was unusual, that on July 4th it had snowed. I tried to picture the infinite flat expanse of white and recalled Siberia. We didn't stay long, though I had the feeling John would have liked us to linger.

Back in the air I thought about Vera and how I'd valued meeting her. She led a simple existence but seemed content. By talking about hunting and berry-picking, she painted a picture of her small community. While I looked out over the vast terrain, I imagined the nomadic way of life her people had led before they settled, so different from my German tradition. Architectural landmarks, castles, cathedrals are my cultural heritage. The Nunamiut people revere a landscape, a river, a mountain. And the caribou have such importance that the word infiltrates their language and existence. I later read the longest word in Inuvialuktun, spoken by the people in Tuktoyaktuk is, "tuktusiuriagatigitqingnapin'ngitkiptin'nga" (I never go caribou hunting with you again).

I wondered about Vera's future. Would I ever know how life treated her? Sudden severe turbulence roused me from my thoughts. My purse and camera flew up and down. I grabbed them and tried to hold on. Despite Ian's seatbelt, his head hit an air vent on the ceiling, which gave him a bloody cut. The airplane kept bouncing, its wings thumping under the wind's force. I lay sideways on the backseat, my feet on the floor, my eyes closed, praying. Please make it stop. Curly said the turbulence wasn't unusual. High winds from variable directions were the culprit. I didn't know then that we were flying south through the Atigun Pass, known among pilots for its severe wind conditions and the difficulties for small planes. The turbulence seemed to last forever, thirty, maybe forty minutes. I worried the fuselage would break apart. Ian told me to remain calm and hang tight. Later that evening, after we'd landed safely, he admitted a broken fuselage had crossed his mind.

Now twenty years later, I've reconnected with Vera over the Internet. She is still as attractive as I remember.

From email I learned that she married twice, divorced, and has only daughters. Outside of her family, Vera is a church elder, a council member for the local school, and a board member of the statewide Museum Association and Native Regional Corporation.

Geography of Alaska

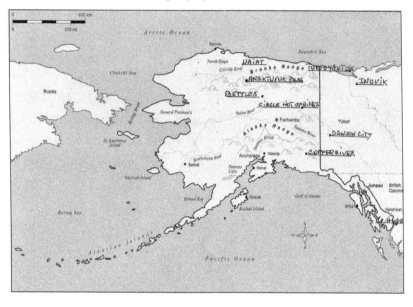

The world is a book, and those who do not travel read only a page.
Saint Augustine

I now ask my readers to move ahead to the 9th of September when Ian and I boarded a ferry boat in Prince Rupert, British Columbia. Our destination was Port Hardy on the northern tip of Vancouver Island, a ride of seventeen hours. We'd awakened before sunrise that morning and driven the bus and car, separately, onto the ferry. A misty rain fell, the air chilly, and low clouds hung over the offshore isles. Later in the day, once the rain stopped, Ian and I took a seat on the outside deck. The boat cruised through gray blue waters, passing rocky islets and hillsides of conifers that grew to the shoreline. The scenery, though beautiful, did not present the thrill of glaciers, emerald blue lakes, and the uninhabited mountain ranges we'd admired the past few months. Yet the sober blue and dark green hues had a calming effect. Lost in our own thoughts, we said little. Our ferry passed a fishing trawler. We waved. I asked Ian if he'd ever considered a boat instead of the bus. No, he was pleased with his choice of vehicle. He liked boating, but land travel offered more variety. I agreed and admitted that my initial reservation about our nomadic existence had proved unfounded. Did he recall the negative comments from friends and acquaintances before our departure? *How do you know where to go? What about your family? How can you leave them? What about holidays?*

"People thought we were abandoning our family," I said.

"Ridiculus," Ian said. "Even if we had a permanent residence, we wouldn't see them on a regular basis."

"We defied those who bet we couldn't last more than three months on a bus," I said, chuckling.

"Because I'm so tolerant."

"No doubt, that's why!" I recollected some of our initial mishaps: mechanical failures, the refrigerator unloading, the trash compactor. Ian grinned. The events seemed funny now. Over the course of a year, we'd adjusted to life on the road, our small accommodations, and now knew when to give each other space. But above all, we hadn't lost our sense of adventure. The windshield of the bus was a window to the world, the open road our village, and people we met along the way our community.

In the days ahead, we planned to slowly venture south to Victoria, indulge in city life, eat dinner out, see a show, and dress in something other than outdoor wear. Ian had suggested high tea at the Empress Hotel and urged me to make a reservation. Another ferry would take us back to the United States, to Port Angeles on the Olympic Peninsula, and places farther south. In late October we planned to be in the Outer Banks of North Carolina to reunite with two of Ian's 1953 classmates from flight school. We would be renting a house together on the beach. I'd already booked a roundtrip from Portland, Oregon, to Richmond, Virginia. And our children, Alec and Natasha, would join us for Christmas in Reno. And in January Ian hoped to take the bus down the Baja Peninsula into Mexico before heading north the following spring. I couldn't foresee an end to our travels.

Around 11 p.m. the ferry docked at Port Hardy. By the time we left the boat, it was raining, the town in darkness. I remembered how frustrated we'd been in Newfoundland the evening we drove off the ferry and couldn't find the motel. This time I drove the car ahead of the bus and hoped to locate the RV park. Heavy rain pounded the windshield, making it impossible to read street names and signs. As I passed unknown roads with the bus's headlights in my rearview mirror, I wondered if we were driving in circles, and mentioned this to Ian via our walkie-talkies. The directions I'd written down didn't make sense. To this day I don't know how we found the RV park. Like the summer of 1999 in Newfoundland, we stumbled on the place by accident.

Every city has a sex and an age which has nothing to do with demography.
John Berger

The city of Victoria is feminine. Attractive and stately, she bears no resemblance to any of the towns we visited the summer of 2000. Anchorage and Fairbanks, both rugged and hardy, had masculine appeal. Seattle seemed a jumpy, restless colt, while Whitehorse, the capital of the Yukon, was a bit feminine, though less spirited, like an older mare. But Victoria was young and lively. Adorned with an array of floral arrangements, she looked particularly lovely under a sunny sky. Her close affiliation with British culture charmed me: the neo-classical architecture, the opera house, the Royal British Museum of Natural History, even the statue of Queen Victoria in front of the British Columbia Parliament Buildings.

We spent over a week in Victoria: sightseeing, shopping, and receiving medical treatments. I'd developed a rash around my mid-rift. Unresponsive to home remedy, the itching gave me sleepless nights. A doctor diagnosed scabies, an illness usually associated with uncleanliness. Tiny microbes had burrowed under my skin. *How could that be, Miss clean Ilona?* We assumed the culprit was an unclean laundry room. The remedy? To smear an anti-parasite solution all over my body from neck to toes, and leave it on for 12 hours, and to wash all bedding, towels, and clothes with which I'd been in contact. Oddly the little pests hadn't invaded Ian, though he harbored a different parasite, later diagnosed as a stubborn blastocyst in his intestines. While I was cured after two treatments, Ian's bug was more difficult to eradicate. He was convinced the source was contaminated water we'd put onboard in a remote location.

Still, we didn't let the ailments spoil our stay. For the first time since the beginning of our journey, I shopped for clothes to replace a few tops and two worn-out pair of corduroys and khakis. Ian and I visited museums and attended musical performances, which prompted Ian to announce that his *cultural-low-level-warning light* was off. We did go for tea at the Empress Hotel, Ian in a suit and tie, I wearing a dress and high heels. Because we hadn't seen each other in anything but outdoor attire for so long, I felt like a teenager going to the prom. Before stepping off the bus, I'd looked out the window to see if anyone was around. The couple next door were lolling in their lawn chairs, drinks in hand, a dog by their feet. *What would they think? That we were going to a funeral?* Their eyes were on us as we stepped off the bus.

"Taking Miss Daisy to town," Ian said in a loud voice and opened the car door for me.

"Miss Daisy, eh? Have a good time," the man said.

I took my seat and waved at them in regal fashion.

In the hotel's dining room at a reserved table by the window, we indulged in soft-buttered sandwiches filled with cucumber, crab, and egg salad, then ate scones with clotted cream, strawberries, and pastries. The ambiance reminded me of my childhood in Germany. *Nachmittagskaffee* (afternoon coffee) it was called. Tables covered with a white cloth, a budvase with a flower or two, china plates, and silver. A civilized way to spend an afternoon then and now at the Empress. The window provided a view over Victoria's busy inner harbor. Boats came and went, seaplanes landed and took off. In a few days, a ferry would take us out of that port to Port Angeles, Washington, on the

Olympic Peninsula.

Hoping to prolong our visit, I told Ian how much I liked Victoria. What would he say if we made the city our ultimate home? A place to live permanently, after we'd ended our travels. I suggested we check out some real estate. To my surprise, Ian agreed. The size and neatness of Victoria pleased him. And he liked the proximity to water. One reason for our journey was to locate the ideal place to settle. Was this it? The following day, an agent showed us several properties on the water. I took a fancy to a traditional cottage overlooking the Strait of Juan de Fuca.

"I really like it," I said to Ian who seemed interested but not ready to make a hasty decision. That night over dinner we agreed the time wasn't right. We weren't ready to stop traveling. There was so much more to explore, and buying a house would deter us. We vowed to revisit Victoria again in the future. Sadly, we never returned.

Thinking about it now, I try to visualize the sweet cottage, to see myself sitting on its porch and looking out over the sea. But settling in Victoria had been a romantic notion. Life had something else in mind. We ended up moving to the East Coast of the United States, closer to old friends and family.

Every day is a journey, and the journey itself is a home.
Matsuo Basho

On the flight from Chicago to Portland I was tired and would have welcomed an hour or two of sleep. It had been a long day that started in the Outer Banks of North Carolina. Night had set in. Except for several reading lights, the cabin was dark. With slight envy I noticed how Ian, seated across the aisle from me, had dozed off. I marveled how he could sleep like that, upright in an airline seat. The couple next to me, wearing earphones, had their eyes closed. I couldn't get comfortable and looked at my watch. Two more hours. By my calculations, we should be over Montana and eight months from now, our bus would travel on its roads.

Images of the past week came to mind. Ian's reunion with his classmates had been pleasant. Saoud, a former captain for Middle East Airlines, had come with his wife, Nina, from Beirut, Lebanon. The other man, Richard, lived in Charlottesville, Virginia. For a week, we'd rented a house on the beach near Hatteras. I'd marveled how peaceful the area was, devoid of crowds in early November. Ian had entertained his friends with stories of our travels. The bus intrigued them, though neither of them could imagine living permanently in such a vehicle. Like the majority of RV owners at the time, they might consider a short trip in a small camper but would not give up their residences. Why is it, I thought, that people choose permanence over the freedom to travel? Is it fear of the unknown that keeps people tied to their roots? Ian and I were different. We'd broken away from ours a long time ago. And having been uprooted many times since, we believed that home is wherever life's journey leads us. But Ian's classmates hadn't moved away from their places of birth and couldn't understand our infatuation with a nomadic life.

The plane had started its descent into Portland when Ian woke and looked at his watch. Almost 8 p.m. He calculated the time it would take to get back home and wondered if there was anything to eat in the bus. I said there should be eggs and cans of soup. He would settle for scrambled eggs with toast. I only craved our cozy bed.

Thirty-five minutes later, we landed. As the plane taxied to the terminal, the woman seated beside me asked if I was visiting Portland. At the time, before the age of small electronic devices, air travelers often showed an interest in their seatmate's travels. These days, as soon as a plane lands and clears the runway, most people immerse themselves in their cell phones. I remember telling the woman that I was going home, and said my husband and I had returned from North Carolina. She was heading home to Salem, South of Portland, and asked if I had a long drive.

"Half an hour away, at most."

"Where do you live?"

"With my husband on a bus." I pointed to Ian across the aisle. He raised his hand and waved.

"A bus? Where?"

"At an RV park. We travel permanently on a bus."

She turned to her husband, seated by the window. "This couple lives on a bus."

"You don't have a home?" he asked.

"The bus is our home. We've no permanent residence."

"How long have you been doing this?"

I saw Ian lean over to partake in the conversation. He told them we'd been on the road for over a year.

"Where to next?" the man asked.

"To Seattle first, then south to California."

He looked at his wife. "We should do that one day."

"You should. Lots of fun," Ian said.

The wife wanted to know how we received mail, paid bills, stayed in contact with friends. Ian explained how easy it was, how our children visited us, how we saw friends along the way, and how our son Alec forwarded the mail once a month via FedEx. By then we'd arrived at the terminal, and the couple wished us well. I wondered if we'd inspired them, or if they thought we were loonies. Would they take to traveling one day? Even if they had good intentions, chances were they would stay home in retirement. The idea of comfort popped up again. Do people delude themselves that there is comfort in permanency?

Back in the bus, before drifting off to sleep, I counted how many times over the past sixteen months we'd left our mobile home and taken a flight. Twice to New York for dental appointments and visits with Natasha. A party in Chicago, another in Miami, Ian's business trips without me. I'd never minded being alone in the bus. Before I could think of the total number, sleep overcame me.

The following morning we headed north to Seattle. The bus would remain at McChord Air Force Base while we stayed in a downtown hotel. Ian was scheduled to participate in another airline safety audit. On the way, we spent two days near Mt. St. Helens. The area, devoid of visitors late in the season, meant we had the terrain to ourselves. Snow covered the higher elevations and, except for smoke rising from its crater, the mountain appeared innocent under its white blanket. From the visitors center we scanned a lifeless yet beautiful landscape merging with the milk-white sky.

A few charred tree trunks remained of the enormous destruction twenty years earlier. In the distance an elk appeared. Ian wondered what had caused the animal to come here, an area lacking vegetation.

That afternoon we sat on the shores of Coldwater Lake, a body of water created when volcanic debris blocked the flow of Coldwater Creek. Fish had resettled in its clear waters, and a pair of ducks was making a soft landing. Life persevered, defying destruction. Isolated, yet quiet and serene, the place prompted deep thoughts. I said to Ian, "We are powerless over nature, its beauty one moment, then devastation. There is no way to predict life's path. Maybe that's what Matsuo Basho meant by *The Journey itself is a home.*"

"Who's Matsuo Basho?"

"A 17th century Japanese poet."

Ian had never heard of him. I explained that he'd been a master of haiku poetry, three-line poems, with a specified number of syllables, often describing nature. I remarked that people crave permanence, even if it is obvious there is no permanence in life. "Everything is on a journey, Ian. Fish, ducks, wind, snow, earth, the stars. Not even in death does the journey end. But to feel at home on it, one has to stop along the way and cherish the moment."

"I'm glad you're enjoying the moment," Ian laughed. "But you'd better get back to reality. I'm getting cold."

We moved on. A month later, on the Donner Pass, a moment in time seemed eternal, and ironically, I hoped the journey would be over soon.

We always take credit for the good and attribute the bad to fortune.
                                                              Charles Kuralt

Snow? Not again, I thought, outraged that Ian would consider driving through another snowstorm, and this time over the Donner Pass. I couldn't understand his reasoning and called him a stubborn mule. But he remained undeterred. We were at Beale Air Force Base, fifty miles north of Sacramento, California, twelve days before Christmas. Son Alec was scheduled to arrive in Reno three days later, Natasha the following week. I hoped for a less stressful holiday, unlike the one a year ago, and looked forward to skiing Northstar and Squaw Valley. All day long I tried to convince Ian to wait for the storm to pass. The Donner Pass was notorious for extreme snow conditions. But he refused. We set the alarm for 4 a.m. on December 13th. By leaving early, Ian was certain we would make it across the mountain ahead of the snow. For the first time ever I hooked the car to the bus in darkness. As we drove off, I reminded Ian of his promise to never drive through snow again.

"We won't," Ian said, "If we encounter accumulation, we'll return to Beale."

I couldn't bear the thought. Of all the bases where we'd parked, Beale had been the least attractive: prefabricated houses in poor condition, a mediocre gym, a badly-stocked commissary. Drizzling rain and fog had added gloom. I'd hoped to buy three or four Christmas gifts on-line at the RV park's office, but the Internet connection was painfully slow. After one frustrating hour I gave up and resorted to pre-cooking meals. If it hadn't been for the forecast, I would have been happy to leave Beale.

That morning, an hour later, we approached I-80 near Colfax and met light snow.

"Looks like another wrong forecast," I said, my tone derisive. Ian brushed me off as he often did. "We'll be across the mountain before any accumulation."

I'd heard that once before. I felt nervous and couldn't sit still. Twenty minutes later the flurries intensified. I questioned my husband's sanity and said we should go back.

"Where do you want me to turn around?"

I got up and paced. "I don't know. Take the next exit."

"Sit down!" My behavior was annoying him. But I continued pleading. "This doesn't look good. Remember your promise."

By the time we reached 5000 feet, dark clouds were overhead, snow accumulating on the road. The temperature gauge showed seventeen degrees. A gale force wind blew heavy snowflakes at the windshield. An overhead traffic sign warned that chains were required.

"Did you see that?"

"I'm not blind. How do you imagine I get chains now?"

"Maybe we should pull into a rest area and wait?"

"Bullshit. Only another two thousand feet and we're across the summit."

I thought of the blizzard in Texas. The current conditions were worse than what we endured then. At least Texas had flat terrain. I shouted. "You're crazy, totally nuts."

"Shut up and leave me alone. I'm concentrating on the road."

The bus inched up the mountain pass in an eighteen-wheeler's tracks. Even under normal conditions my acrophobia would have caused anxiety. My heart pounded.

"I can't watch this."

"Go to bed."

"I will. Go to hell." I went to the bedroom, took a valium I'd reserved for emergencies, and pulled the bed covers over my head. Let me fall asleep before we run off the road. The bus's engine rumbled, the tires crunched through snow. When sleep didn't come, I dared to peek out from the covers. Flurries whirled outside the bedroom window. Trees on the hillside were covered in white. I lay back down. The bus kept pushing up the mountain. The pill worked and I must have dozed off. Ian's voice awakened me.

"Get up. We made it. Come look at the view."

I heard the bus shift into low gear and walked up front. The road was clear, the sky blue.

"I told you," Ian said.

I said it was easy to take credit with luck on his side.

"No! It's skill." He explained how he'd followed the trucks. Eighteen wheelers in slippery conditions had devices that drop sand in front of their wheels. Later we heard that the highway police had checked every truck for chains.

We arrived at the RV park near Reno. The bus was covered with the highway's grime and dirty sand. The car looked unrecognizable, as if dragged through a muddy river. After Ian had taken the bus to a truck wash and returned, I told him that I would never again cross the Donner Pass. He would be on his own getting to California after the holidays. I would fly to San Francisco or Sacramento. He could meet me there. Ian assured me that we would stay in Reno as long as necessary after the holidays for the roads to dry before driving back. We never drove through snow again.

And now we welcome the New Year, full of things that have never been.
Rainer Maria Rilke

Fireworks over Reno announced 2001. To watch the display, Ian, Natasha and I drove to a hill west of town. Alec had already flown back to Daytona. Below in the valley, multicolored neon lights defined the city, darkness concealed the surrounding areas before the show began. It was cold that night, a dry cold, and no wind. The few people gathered around us were bundled in winter gear. We didn't leave the car until the first rockets shot into the sky.

"Best seats in town," Ian commented as Roman candles discharged golden stars, followed by sparkling trails of chrysanthemums, and long silvery strings in the shape of a weeping willow. Natasha was in awe as a rocket broke into multicolored lights, and long bright shoots formed the outline of giant fiery palms, lighting the entire valley. I'd never watched a more beautiful spectacle. Then it was over. The last few swells of smoke blew over the city before disappearing into the dark sky. Happy New Year.

We couldn't foresee what 2001 would bring. As is customary, we wished each other happiness and good health, unaware of what would befall us a few months later. During our drive back home, pleasant memories from the past year emerged. The few unpleasant ones, I ignored. In one year we'd seen so much of North America,

From The
Globetrotters!
Ian and Ilona Duncan

Happy Holidays
2000

driven to the northern most coastal villages, traveled every road in Alaska, some of them twice, all without an accident. My fears had been unfounded. None of the bridges collapsed, the bus didn't break down in ice and snow, a skilled driver had kept our home safe and unharmed, particularly on some treacherous roads. And, unlike the previous year, Christmas had been peaceful. I'd even prepared our traditional Christmas Eve dinner in the bus: Beef Wellington with Madeira sauce. Alec, my gourmet son, had insisted I try it. Otherwise Christmas Eve wouldn't be the same, he'd said. The roast had turned out surprisingly well. Had the food made a difference? Maybe we had lower expectations this year. Although the bus could never gain favorite status for Christmas ambiance, we'd accepted it as our domicile for enjoying the holiday together.

The following morning over coffee, I asked Ian if the past year on the bus had turned out the way he hoped. Given the chance, would he do things differently? Nothing he could think of. He wondered if I had any regrets. I thought about this for a moment, then said that I should have purchased more mammoth tusk carvings in Dawson City, the only ivory allowed for importation to the United States, and that Navajo rug regardless of the cost. Much as I didn't care about possessions, I thought they would be future mementos of our journey. Especially I regretted not acquiring more burl wood bowls at a roadside shack in the Yukon and told Ian about this. Beautifully crafted, they would have made great future gifts, I said.

"Why didn't you?"

"I was in a hurry. You didn't like to stop there."

Ian reminded me the place was on the opposite side of the Alaska Highway, the parking area too narrow, which meant backtracking twenty miles to turn the bus around.

"A little detour. Why the big deal?"

"Because you don't understand what it's like driving the bus. And

I always concede to Miss Daisy's whims."

I asked Ian what he thought had been the biggest nuisance of our travels. He said that one recurrent hindrance was the vehicle itself. The parking areas were often too small and the electric hook-up insufficient. Most RV and state parks in 2000, particularly in the remote areas we'd traveled, were not equipped to handle the size of the bus and offered only a fifteen or thirty ampere connection. Ian preferred fifty. We recalled the night near Mount St. Helens when insufficient electrical power caused the lights to go off during dinner. Flashlight in hand, Ian had gone out in the dark to check the connection at the plug-in post and found a tripped circuit breaker that wouldn't reset. Instead of alerting the office of the RV park, we got on our hands and knees, snaked an electric chord underneath the bus to the plug-in of the vacant slot next to us.

"Why didn't we start the generator?"

"Remember, generators are prohibited overnight."

"Who would have complained?" I said, recalling only two or three other vehicles that night. Ian had been surprised it was even open with temperatures below freezing,

"Made for a cozy night under the covers," Ian said and smiled.

I asked if, in hindsight, he would have chosen a smaller vehicle. No, he liked the comfort of ours. I wanted to know what type of electrical connections he expected to find in Europe. He wasn't sure. He mentioned adaptors and high-power electrical converters. Taking the bus across the Atlantic was at least a year away, so I didn't inquire further.

Natasha flew back to New York on January 2nd. As usual, I was sad that our children were once again so far away. Ian and I traveled south. We chose the coastal route with stops in Salinas, Carmel, and Santa Barbara, before reaching San Diego. From there Ian hoped to drive the bus south through the Baja peninsula to Cabo San Lucas, but I wondered if Mexico would be safe. The following summer we planned to drive north again, through Utah, and Montana to Manitoba.

One evening over dinner I asked Ian where he thought we would spend the following winter. He said it would be somewhere south of Arkansas. Louisiana maybe, or Texas. From there we would have to carefully choose our timing. We needed to arrive in Boston in the spring of 2002 to prepare the bus for shipping it across the Atlantic to a port in Scandinavia. Ian had already contacted several shipping companies for price quotes. He'd been assured that we could travel along with our rig on the same cargo ship. Another adventure, but first Ian had to get well.

A bend in the road is not the end of the road, unless you fail to make the turn.
Helen Keller

Ian waited until we arrived in San Diego to see another rheumatologist. The doctor was shocked to learn Ian had been taking prednisone for a year and hesitated to treat him. After an unsettling moment of silence, the doctor gazed intently at Ian and said he had a condition called rheumatoid arthritis.

"You must stay in town for four to five months if you want me to help you."

"Ouch." This word had come out against my will.

"Why ouch?" he asked.

"We are nomads. It's going to hurt, staying that long in one place."

Maybe, the doctor said, but he saw no other way for Ian to recover.

We'd arrived in San Diego toward the end of January 2001, just prior to my fifty-sixth birthday. Five months? Until July? Ian had hoped to be in Montana by then. We left the office without saying a word, lost in our thoughts. Driving home, Ian was the first to break the silence.

"I have two choices."

"Which are?"

"We stop traveling for good, or stay under the care of this doctor for the time being."

I understood what he was trying to tell me. He'd already made a decision and accepted his fate without complaint. The prednisone had caused his health to deteriorate. He had the onset of glaucoma, high blood pressure, weight gain, liver damage, and high blood sugar. But worse, his unpredictable mood swings alarmed me. One minute he could be fired up and depressed the next.

I rationalized that we could be in a worse place. We'd visited San Diego several times in the past. The city is a treat for art lovers, has wonderful restaurants, and many theaters. Besides, with its beautiful beaches, glorious sunsets over the Pacific, and snow-capped mountains to the east, San Diego is one of the more attractive places in the United States. And there were several military bases where we could park the bus. Not only were the bases less costly, they usually offered a nicer and more spacious setup. But to minimize permanent residents, these campgrounds usually limited a stay to two weeks. We chose to shuttle back and forth between the Naval Amphibious Base at Fiddler's Cove on the beach of Coronado, to Miramar Marine Corps Air Station, twenty miles north.

Without travel, our daily routine took on a slower pace, and before long old habits resurfaced. Instead of reading the checklist before our morning departure, we read the newspaper, Ian at the dinette table, I in the bedroom. In lieu of studying a map, Ian took his time evaluating the stock market and studying financial news. And without the morning rush for an on-time departure, we finished the crossword puzzle together, taking turns with the answers. We recalled how we'd started the practice years ago, working the New York Times puzzle together. Ian had the advantage then because of my inadequate English vocabulary.

Some days, we went for a walk, on others to the gym. Both military bases had well-equipped exercise facilities that offered various work-out routines and yoga. Except for a few household chores and driving to medical appointments, we had excessive idle time. More than ever I cooked and baked. On several occasions, we observed the Navy Seals exercising from the beach at Fiddler's Cove. Some afternoons, for a change of scenery, I went with Ian to the golf range. A book in hand, I glanced up now and then to watch his swing and see where the balls landed. Ian even played the occasional round after he'd befriended other golfers. At last the golf bag with its array of clubs came into full use.

Ian still hoped to take the bus to Mexico for a week or two, to drive south on the Baja peninsula, if not all the way to Cabo. Yet the cost to insure the bus and car in Mexico crushed his plan. USAA, our regular insurance carrier, refused coverage and suggested we contact a local company in San Diego. The Yellow Pages showed a number of agencies that advertised Mexican auto insurance. Ian called one after another to hear, *"We're happy to insure the car, but the bus – no señor."* Hijacking was their fear. Yet Ian persisted. Only one company would guarantee a safe passage for both vehicles, at the fee of one hundred dollars per day. I didn't think I heard right when Ian mentioned the cost.

"Three thousand a month?"

"Yes, three thousand. Obviously we're not going."

"For that amount we could fly to Cabo and stay in a hotel for a few days."

But Ian wasn't interested in flying there. We'd done that twice before, in the 1980s. His idea was to explore a different part of the peninsula. We never went. Instead we made a few daytrips to Tijuana. The town held little interest, but we located a good dentist who spoke excellent English.

As the weeks went on, I sensed how unhappy we'd become, having never relished idleness. Although the surroundings were pleasant, there was little to do. I spent hours with books and finished a needlepoint pillow. We rented movies to watch in the evenings. The bus had lost its purpose. I thought of people who park their moto-rhomes in one place for an entire season. I couldn't imagine. To remain in one location, Ian and I needed a community. Even our neighbors were transitory. For the first time Ian lamented that our children lived so far away. And he wished for the camaraderie of old friends, workmates, familiar golf club buddies. I missed my piano. Since childhood music had been an intrinsic part of my life. I'd filled hours of otherwise idle time at the keyboard. And now I longed for the melancholy of a Chopin nocturne, the beauty of a Mozart or Bee-thoven sonata, the glory of a Bach prelude. Was there a way to obtain permission to play the organ in one of the churches?

One morning, for lack of anything else to do, I felt the urge to clean out closets and fill a bag with donations. I opened the sliding doors in back of our bed's headboard and slid out the clothes rack. An old suit reminded me of the times we'd entertained business acquain-tances. Would I ever wear it again? And the long silk skirt? Would I ever dress up? Unlikely. Once I'd reorganized the bedroom's closets, I wanted to look inside the trunks in the under-floor compartment and asked Ian to help me lift them out. He didn't see the point and said they contained clothes we'd never needed. But I insisted. Ian knew better than to argue once my cleaning craze took hold. Similar to a woman who scrubs her kitchen before going into labor, I couldn't be stopped. Reluctantly he opened the compartment and hoisted two trunks onto the picnic table under the awning.

"Let's see what we find in here," Ian said and lifted the lids.

The smell of mothballs hit us. I covered my nostrils with one hand and fanned the fumes with the other.

"For sure no larvae or pests have survived in there," Ian said, a wide grin on his face.

I admitted that I'd misjudged the amount of mothballs. Ian

thought it was funny. "With that stink we'll kill every moth within a three mile radius."

The pungent odor had permeated every garment. Ian suggested airing them out. Where was I was supposed to do that, I asked.

"Put the clothes on hangers and hang them from the awning."

How tacky, I thought. "What will our neighbors think?"

"Since when do you care about neighbors?"

No sooner were the garments dangling outside the bus, than a slight breeze carried the pungent, sickly-sweet smell to a neighbor, who began waving her arms to fan away the odor.

"Our neighbors took notice. They can smell the moth balls."

"It'll be gone in no time," Ian shrugged.

It wasn't. A week later the clothes still hadn't given up their nasty smell. A professional cleaner eventually took care of the garments.

In mid-March I begged Ian to take me for a day to Borrego Springs and the blooming desert of the Anza-Borrego State Park. He wasn't keen on making a four-hour roundtrip to see, as he put it, a bunch of flowers.

"It's wildlife."

"Not what I consider wildlife."

"A desert flower is wild and alive," I said, and there might be some animals as well.

"Yes, scorpions and snakes," Ian said.

He'd never understood my love of flowers, in particular wild flowers. I told him that they were food for the soul. Ian said not to forget how often he stopped the car so I could take one more photo of some flower. I'd appreciated his patience, I said. But instead of a photo, I wished I'd collected a single bloom of each one: Blue forget-me-nots, pink moss campions, purple shooting stars, arctic lupine, and blue geraniums, a lovely collection of pressed flowers in a book. Ian said I should have been a botanist.

Reluctantly he agreed to drive me to the State Park. As if by magic, nature had decorated the drab, desolate, and rocky terrain with yellow brittlebush, purple desert sand verbenas, white and pink desert primroses. In view of such rare beauty, my spirits lifted and, for a few hours, all worries were forgotten.

The euphoria didn't last. Back in San Diego, the bus had another break-down. During one of our repositioning drives Ian noticed the engine wasn't producing enough power and took it at once to a specified repair facility. I followed in the car. A mechanic diagnosed a broken piston rod. The engine needed disassembling, which would take more than a week at the cost of several thousand dollars. Ian took the news better than I.

"Simple maintenance," he said, "Just like house expenses. Not any different than roof repair and a house painting."

I was aghast and said the bus has turned into a money pit. Ian said to take everything of value off the bus, that we were moving to a hotel.

Ten days later the bus was repaired, and we moved back in. Weeks went by. Ian underwent one medical procedure after another. Had there been a customer loyalty program at the Scripps Medical Center and hospital, he would have reached gold status. At times I wondered if Ian would ever be well again. Was this the end of our journey? The end of life? We'd been young and fit. Now aging and sickness was a reality. And the two only lead to one final destination. Death. A somber thought.

On Mother's Day, the 13th of May, I had cabin fever. I missed my children. Natasha had recently made the cover of Mode magazine.

When she'd told us, we'd immediately rushed to get copies, several of them. Ian proudly showed her photo to the office workers
at Miramar's RV park. *That's your daughter? No way.* I wanted her
nearby, but had to console myself with her photos. I again picked
up the magazine and studied her beautiful face framed by long red,
naturally curly hair. She'd been a model for only a year, though acting
was her primary goal. Yet she'd made a name for herself in the fashion world.

That night I had one of my recurrent dreams about a house, in
which the house burns down. Somewhere I'd read that a house in
dreams symbolizes the inner life of the dreamer. I attributed the
dream to my current senseless existence, shuttling between two RV
parks. I missed family life, a regular home where our children could
visit. In my diary, I described the phase of my life as limited, meaningless, boring, and depressing. My entries turned philosophical: We
delude ourselves with the notion that we are in charge of our destiny.
We are powerless when it comes to natural disasters and illness.
Even Ian had lost his sense of humor. We discussed where we could
settle if his medical situation didn't improve. San Diego didn't feel
right. Though we knew our way around town, had favorite restau-

rants, attended theatrical performances, we didn't want to settle in Southern California. Instead, I imagined a small cottage surrounded by trees and flowers, a place where I could see crocus bloom and hear birds sing in spring, where I would enjoy the lazy days of a warm summer, admire the colorful foliage in fall, and where snow-flakes would adorn the countryside in winter.

A short visit by Natasha brought a reprieve. She came to spend Father's Day with Ian. I admired her positive outlook on life. *Life is a gift that should be loved for all it offers*, she told me. *Joy, sadness, and pain should be embraced because it means being alive.* On the 18th of June we drove her to Los Angeles airport for her flight back to New York. As we parted, I saw in her face the most contagious, catching smile. I will never forget how happy she looked, as she walked into the terminal.

By the end of June, Ian had responded well to his new medica-tions, had lost twenty pounds, and felt better. I was relieved to see him smile and once again find humor in life. And, except for peri-odic blood and liver checks, he was free to travel. Ian didn't waste a moment. With great enthusiasm he studied maps. How soon could we reach Yellowstone Park and Montana? He hoped to be in Manito-ba no later than August, and anticipated traveling into lesser known territory and making the train journey to Churchill, a town on the

Hudson Bay, famous for its polar bear population. It sounded like another exciting voyage to the remote North. Yet I was cautious not to be overly enthusiastic. Was fear of disappointment the reason I didn't share Ian's high expectations? Was Ian really well enough to continue? We'd agreed to fly back to San Diego in the fall for a follow-up visit with the rheumatologist. What other obstacle could impair us? On the eve of our departure from San Diego, I tried to make sense of my worries. Then I recalled the words of Deepak Chopra: *Use memories, but don't let memories use you.* I pushed the dark thoughts away and focused on the good times of the previous year.

A real voyage in discovery consists not in seeking new landscapes
but in having new eyes.
Marcel Proust

With my feet tapping the rhythm, I rocked from side to side and sang along with Roy Orbison. Ooby Dooby, Ooby Dooby. Ian turned the sound of the CD to full blast and chimed in: doo wah, doo wah, doo wah.

"Happy to be back on the road?" I asked.

"Elated."

That morning, June 30th, we'd left San Diego early, two years to the date we'd left Florida. I'd felt mixed emotions then. But now, after many idle months, Ian and I acted like silly teenagers despite the scorching heat in the Mojave Desert. The bus struggled to climb the mountain passes. We stopped numerous times to keep the engine from overheating and kept the air conditioning off to conserve power.

"I can't understand why anyone wants to live here," Ian said, wiping sweat from his face.

"I suppose you want to settle in Canada?" I asked.

"Sounds better every day."

"What about the flies and mosquitos there?"

"They don't bother me as much as this heat."

"I'll get some ice from the freezer," I said, recalling the summer of 1966 when a friend and I traveled the same route by car without air-conditioning. We'd used ice cubes then to cool us off. While I rubbed ice over Ian's forehead, neck, and arms, I mentioned how grueling it must have been for people before the invention of air-conditioning. Ian responded that no sane individual would be living in this part of the world. With both air-conditioning systems running at full speed, the bus had barely enough time to cool down during an overnight stop in Las Vegas. The following day, crossing into Utah, the bus overheated again. To lessen the load, I unhooked the car and prepared to drive it. Slightly envious, Ian told me to enjoy the cool air. In tandem we reached Zion Canyon an hour and a half later. Ian was covered in sweat as he stepped off the bus.

"This is a hell hole."

"No, it's Southern Utah in the summer," I said. At one hundred degrees outside, the interior of the bus felt like a sauna.

"We could have been farther north by now." I heard a tone of regret and listened about how doubtful he'd been the past few months regarding our future travel. I suggested that we cool off in the shower, go out for dinner, and let the A/C units do their job.

Still the heat didn't deter us from staying a few days to tour the area by car and admire the many red, orange, and yellow limestone formations. On our way to Bryce Canyon, the road climbed eight hundred feet to the entrance of the Zion Mount Carmel Tunnel. As usual, I'd become anxious at the sight of the many switchbacks and closed my eyes during the ascent.

"You should have seen the scenery," Ian said.

"I'm sure it was amazing."

"You'll get a chance next time."

"What next time?"

"When you drive the car." The emphasis was on you.

"You're not serious. You want me to drive the car up here? Why?"

"The bus can't get through the hairpin turns with the car in tow."

"Can't we take another road?"

"Not unless you want to add eighty miles to the journey."

"I don't care. I'm not driving the car up that road."

"What's the big deal? A few hairpin curves."

Ian didn't give me a choice. The day he drove the bus up the mountain, I followed closely. Without guard rails, the road curved in serpent-like fashion. I didn't dare to look up or down, clutched the steering wheel and focused on the rear of the bus. "You can do this." I repeated the words aloud, until the bus stopped halfway in a tight hairpin and dropped a few feet back. My foot on the brake, I felt my entire body stiffen with fright. For a moment it seemed as if I were dangling in a Ferris wheel in mid-air. *Please let this be over soon.* I took a deep breath. The bus continued uphill. The thought of taking a photo came to mind. *Would I dare to open the window?* I grabbed the camera from the passenger seat, took a quick shot through the windshield. When I stepped out of the car at the entrance of the tunnel, my legs were wobbly.

"How was it?" Ian asked, the usual incorrigible grin on his face.

"The highlight of my life. What do you think?"

"You did well. I knew you could do it."

A permit and police escort were required to drive the bus through the tunnel. Traffic had to be stopped both ways. A Park Ranger led the way. Ian followed, keeping the bus on the centerline to avoid hitting the rounded ceiling. I trailed behind. After exiting the tunnel, we stopped at the first possible turnoff, hooked the car back to the bus, and continued through Southern Utah, passing giant colorful boulders interspersed with desert shrubs and Ponderosa pines. In the days ahead Ian and I boated around Lake Powell, and I walked the narrow passageway between 4000 feet high spiraling limestone walls in Antelope Canyon. And, as I had in 1966, I admired the dry, mysterious beauty of Monument Valley and commented that few artists could create what nature paints so well. Every bit of scenery filled me with wonder. Fears and concerns of the past months slowly moved into a deeper sphere of memory. What was there to worry about? Our children were well. Alec was approaching his final year at Embry-Riddle University. The older sons were successful, the grandchildren healthy, and Natasha was about to finish acting school in New York City and join a theater company. She'd recently had dinner with her older brother Jim who was surprised how beautiful she'd become. Ian and I were at peace and greeted each new day as if it were a gift. The bus was operating well. There was little to argue about. Even the lack of cellphone coverage didn't cause distress. I welcomed Ian's nonchalant demeanor. Unlike the beginning of our journey, he now surrendered to the spontaneity of the moment.

"Let's keep on traveling forever," I said to Ian one evening.

"You mean on the bus?"

"Yes, I don't ever want to stop."

Ian smiled from ear to ear. "You're glad I talked you into it then?"

"Eternally grateful."

We opted to stay two days in Bluff, a tiny community in southeastern Utah. The RV park was empty except for a lone tent. Ian wondered about the lack of visitors. I blamed the heat, Ian the economy. Early that evening, we'd just finished dinner, an eerie twilight illuminated the limestone ridge to the south. Dark clouds announced a storm. Following a momentary rain shower, a double rainbow formed, its colorful arches stretching far across the valley.

"They say that there's gold at the end of a rainbow," I said, and stepped off the bus for a better view.

"You better run and get it." Ian had come up behind me.

"You, too. We each take one."

"I don't need any gold."

"I don't either."

"My gold is right here," Ian said and put his arms around me.

For a short moment, a warm feeling arose. I asked Ian if he knew any aphorism with regard to a double rainbow. He didn't but thought that such a unique occasion had to be a good omen. We took a seat at a picnic table. I said for ages rainbows had fascinated people, every religion with its own interpretation, mostly good ones. Though not based on logical thinking, they were beautiful mythical tales. Ian said a rainbow is a simple weather phenomenon. But I had grown up with superstition. As a child, Mother used to warn me not to spill salt because it would result in a fight within the family. And God forbid if I should break a mirror. Seven years of bad luck. I'd read somewhere that a double rainbow symbolizes transformation, and mentioned this to Ian. I said in Chinese culture a double rainbow announces a change from the material to the spiritual world. Nonsense, he thought. Old wives' tales. Distant thunder put an end to our pondering. The rainbow disappeared, we went inside. After the sun had set, lightening flashed across the nocturnal sky. We sat in the dark to better admire the display of nature's fury until rain pounded on the roof and thunder faded in the distance. In the morning we awakened to the pungent odor of sagebrush.

A week later, on July 18th, we were driving the car through Southwestern Wyoming with the hope of taking a video of wild horses, running freely the way I'd observed in movies. But the small herds we saw appeared lazy and tame. With a hope to get the horses moving, I stepped out of the car twice, shouted at them, clapped my hands. Yet the horses remained undeterred, looked at me for a brief moment, and continued munching on the dry grasses.

Ian was ready to move on. "Are you done with your photo?"

"No, I want to see them running."

"I don't think they want to."

"Can't you do something?"

"What do you want me to do?"

"Chase them."

"Anything to please Miss Daisy," Ian mumbled, stepped from the car, walked toward the herd and shouted giddy-up. But the horses trotted only few feet away.

"You need to scare them."

"How?"

"Scream. Throw something. Run after them." In the video, Ian ended up the star of the show, not the horses.

Later that same week, the evening of Saturday July 21st, our lives changed forever. We'd arrived in Casper the day before. I anticipated going to the annual Beartrap Music Festival on Casper Mountain. There would be a variety of live music with several Blue Grass groups and the Wyoming Symphony Orchestra.

The sun shone brightly the afternoon we arrived at Beartrap Meadow, a natural theater. Country music reverberated from a tented stage overlooking a wide meadow, tall pines and conical spruces on either side. People with picnics had gathered on blankets. Children were dancing to the rhythms of the songs. We walked a few feet downhill, away from the stage, and spread a towel under the shade of a pine tree. Pleased with the location, I told Ian that, in a symphony hall, our seats would be in the left orchestra section. I lay down, closed my eyes, and thanked my good fortune. Images from the past two weeks came to mind. The Great Salt Lake had been disappointing. We'd gone for a picnic at Silver Sands Beach where I'd hoped once again to recline in the salty waters, unable to sink as I did in 1966. But the waters had receded to expose a muddy shoreline. Canyonlands had been a pleasant surprise. As a souvenir I kept a small bouquet of rose-heath to dry. And I wondered when if ever, I would display the Navajo rug I'd bought in Moab, the same one I'd considered too expensive the year before in Arizona. The music stopped. Except for the light chatter of people, there was silence. A neighbor noticed we had not brought food and offered their fare. Though I was touched by the kindness, we declined. At 6:30, the symphony orchestra started playing a piece by Wagner. How odd I thought. Wagner in Wyoming. The sounds of multiple reeds and brass resonated down the tree-lined meadow. I thought of Natasha. The bucolic setting reminded me of a recent conversation with her. She and I had spoken about the spiritual power of nature and its effect on people. She'd told me that often she felt God's presence when surrounded by nature's beauty. And if ever she were to marry, she would prefer an outside ceremony on a hill with trees and wild flowers. I thought Beartrap Meadow fit that description. The concert ended with a piece by Belioz. The music transported my senses to dreamlike spheres where reality and imagination become one. Ian and I did not know that in those early evening hours, almost two thousand miles away in New York City, our daughter drew her last breath. And with her death, our love affair with the bus came to a sudden end.

Twenty years from now you will be more disappointed by the things you didn't do than by the ones you did do.
Mark Twain

Now, almost twenty years later, Ian and I share happy memories of our adventures. During the course of our journey, we'd set out to explore unfamiliar territories and to meet diverse people. Despite misunderstandings, illnesses, and conflicts, we shared a love for each other and a curiosity for the unknown. The bus was the home we took on a long vacation, a venture that differed from any taken before. Except for the few days of our children's visits, and Ian's brief business trips, we'd spent every hour, day after day, over 800 in total, alone in each other's company. The amount of days may seem a long time. In our case, 800 days were too short. And, contrary to our friends' prediction that our togetherness would be disastrous, we grew closer.

I fondly recall some of the people we met during our travels: Cynthia in Gloucester whose husband had died of an overdose, and Anne, the mortician, who invited me to eat cheesecake with blueberries. I wonder if Mark, the hitchhiker in Labrador, ever found peace within himself, and if Simon, the spirited young guide in Tuktoyaktuk, learned a third language. And I will never forget beautiful Vera in Anaktuvuk who was so proud of her village and history. But most people we encountered were other travelers, strangers on the road, who showed an interest in our vehicle. The bus, our *omnibus nobis* was the star. The minute we entered an RV Park, a crowd gathered. Young and old wanted a tour, lines formed at the front door. And for the children, Miss Daisy always had a treat to hand out.

The northern lands remain embedded in my memory. I read that Tuktoyuktuk is growing. Since the fall of 2018, a highway connects it to Inuvik. People don't have to wait for the ground to be frozen to make the drive in winter. Yet I've also read that climate change has caused the pingos to disappear and the whales to arrive earlier. Still I hope continuous exploration and global warming won't destroy the region's beauty, and that the venturesome traveler who makes the 600-mile-journey from Dawson City to Tuktoyaktuk will treasure the peacefulness and splendor as we did in the year 2000.

If I had to choose one element that made our journey unique, I would say it was freedom. Like most people's lives, ours had been organized by schedules, most of which were beyond our control. For years, from the moment we awakened to the hour we fell asleep, we had to keep check of time. As children we obeyed the school hours, the meal times, and the deadline for returning home. Later, as adults, employment demanded a schedule, and life as a family had rules and an agenda. Even a vacation required a timetable and a set etiquette. More recently, the Internet and social media have added further restrictions on freedom and privacy. Our bus provided a unique opportunity to organize our own lives. For 800 days, Ian and I shared a close intimacy with each other and the environment. We discovered the spiritual and uplifting beauty in nature. *Aus der Natur, nach welcher Seite hin man schaue, entspringt Unendliches.* (From nature, whichever way one looks, leaps the eternal) I'd read Goethe's words by accident in the beginning of our journey. Now I understand them. To see nothing but mountains, rivers, and forest for miles on end is to see nature's eternal soul. And there, amidst the enormity of creation we felt so small, not more important than the green needle on a black spruce.

Our home was the journey. Home was the lonely road and the highway, the rivers and valleys, the desert and the meadow with Arctic cotton. Home was the blizzard, the disputes, the blunders, the illness, the sadness, and the joy. Home was the journey few people have taken and many should. Together we faced the challenge of the day, enjoyed the beauty of the moment, and felt the mystery of love.

The circumstances of our daughter's death remain a mystery. The last time I saw Natasha, at the Los Angeles Airport, she'd been a happy young woman, full of life. After her memorial service in New York City, and a preliminary settlement of her estate, Ian and I flew back to Wyoming, and returned to the bus. The day we prepared to leave the RV park, Ian said he couldn't continue with our travels. He'd lost interest in Yellowstone Park, Montana, Canada. My sense of adventure had vanished, too. The beautiful scenery had lost its appeal. Like somnambulists, Ian and I headed south in silence, passing through Colorado, Kansas, Georgia, without taking notice. The bus, too small for a grieving couple, had to go. We unloaded it in Daytona. A year later our home on wheels had a new owner.

There were times in the months following Natasha's passing when Ian and I lost interest in life. Still, we hoped not to lose each other. Some traditions talk about beauty in death because it eventually nourishes life. For a long time, we couldn't see beauty in either. I regret not having taken the bus to Europe, although driving the narrow country roads and passing through small villages may have posed a bigger challenge than we'd anticipated. Still, I'd reasoned that we were not different than a tour bus that conquers the roads between Scandinavia and the Mediterranean. And though friends suggested that we try again, in a smaller vehicle, we didn't believe in re-opening a chapter of life that had closed.

Our journey had changed us as individuals and as a couple. Life had taken a new meaning. We recognized how nonessential material possessions were. And the closeness we experienced forced us to see our differences and accept them, thereby strengthening our relationship. People deal with tragedy in different ways. Many couples separate after such an event. Without our journey, the sudden heartbreak of our daughter's death might have destroyed our marriage. Yet after living for months on the bus, we'd developed a deeper trust toward each other. We felt each other's pain, knew how to give each other space in the days of mourning and understood when to reach out for help. There were times, Ian wanted to give up life, and there were times I saw no reason to continue. Yet we had each other's support and gave each other hope.

Afterword from the Author

That August of 2001, three weeks after Natasha's death, Ian and I spent the night in a Kansas RV park. Sleep was sporadic and we rose before dawn. With a coffee in hand, I went outside, sat at a picnic table, lit a cigarette, and stared into the darkness. Both Ian and I were smoking again. Sunk in sorrow, he and I did not speak. No words eased our pain. In silence we drank our coffee.

In recent weeks, a whirlwind of emotions had struck us. First the phone call, followed by the flight to New York City, police, identification of our daughter, the memorial. More than three hundred people came to celebrate Natasha's life. How could they not have loved her? She was beautiful, kind, funny, sincere, talented. The phrase *we're sorry for your loss* resonated. We heard it hundreds of times, accepted the words with gracious nods. Yet the sympathetic overtures barely registered. Ian and I had not reached the stage of anger and remorse. We were both numb.

Feeling as if I hadn't slept in days, and in need of more coffee, I went inside the bus, refilled our cups, returned, and sat again. In the early morning stillness, I lit another cigarette and blew smoke into the air. Not a light anywhere. People still asleep in their campers. As soon as the sun rose, Ian and I would be on the road, though not as before, with excitement about what the day might bring.

Then suddenly, out of the darkness, a cat appeared. At a slow but steady pace, the cat walked toward me until it reached my feet. Then it jumped into my lap, sat back on its hind paws, and began to knead—as if making a bed. The cat lifted its head, looked at me, gave a soft meow, and curled into my lap. I saw Ian's dumbfounded look and heard his words. "Unusual for a cat to jump into a stranger's lap. Looks clean and healthy. Who's its owner? Where do you think it came from?"

I sat quietly, stroking the cat's soft black coat, listening to its subtle rhythmic purr, touching its white paws. Natasha's relation with cats had been unique. I remembered her beloved cat, Sonya. She, too, had white paws. Could this cat that came to me out of the darkness be a sign from my daughter? As the cat's eyes closed and she fell asleep, I felt the ache in my heart lessen.

Ian had seized on the moment, too. He felt the cat was a messenger sent to console us. Neither of us dared to move for fear of disturbing this mysterious moment. I can't say how long we sat there. Twenty, maybe thirty minutes. Then dawn illuminated the surroundings and the cat awakened. It looked up at me one last time and jumped down. Without making a sound, the white-pawed cat walked slowly away and disappeared. Still in a daze from this surreal encounter, Ian and I remained seated for many more minutes, convinced the cat was a sign from Natasha.

I'd always been suspicious of supernatural occurrences. The white-pawed cat opened me to a new perception of the mysterious. Natasha had been interested in mysticism and ethnic legends. She'd studied Taoism, Zen and Tibetan Buddhism, read books by Carl Jung and the Dalai Lama. *What was life about? Why are we here, she wanted to know?* In death, had she discovered the answer? And, short of any explanation, my mind and heart opened to inexplicable occurrences and found them consoling.

Months later, ladybugs began visiting me. The French call the little beetle *coccinelle*. It was one of Natasha's nicknames, and the sign-in to her AOL email account. Ladybugs kept appearing in locations that she and I loved. They gathered outside the window on the 30th floor of a high-rise in Manhattan. Others met me inside a Japanese restaurant. Some greeted me at my daughter's favorite store, and a few came to me one day in a train station. Once during a concert, a single *coccinelle* crept across my handbag. In a gift shop in St. Petersburg, Russia, I noticed one sitting on a shelf. Ladybugs followed me to Virginia and joined me in the garden and by our dock. Like the white-pawed cat at an unknown RV park somewhere in Kansas, I welcomed ladybugs as my daughter's messengers, knowing that she is with me always, filling my heart with awe and joy.

Acknowledgements

Sincere thanks to my editor and friend, Gail Kenna, for her vision, patience, hours of encouragement, and belief in my story.

Thanks are also due to Mike Antonio for his expertise with graphics and his help formatting the book.

Special thanks to my writing friends Sharon Baldacci and Marjory Willis whose suggestions and observations helped me improve my narrative.

I am grateful to my husband, Ian, for his love and support during the many hours of writing about our adventure. As my traveling partner, he supplied valuable information, and I often relied on his memory to recall details.

And many thanks to the people who offered help, gave information, or provided companionship and fun during our time on the road.

CPSIA information can be obtained
at www.ICGtesting.com
Printed in the USA
LVHW011350230520
656343LV00005B/339